To Trev,
    with love,
        From Dad
          Christmas 1981

SPITFIRE

A Documentary History

Alfred Price *F.R.Hist.S.*

SPITFIRE

A Documentary History

Macdonald and Jane's · London

Author's Note

The story of the progressive development of the Spitfire from the Mark 1 to the final Mark 24 is a lengthy one and has been covered several times before. It is not intended to relate the story yet again in this book. Readers requiring more detail on individual marks of Spitfire are invited to refer to *Spitfire—the Story of a Famous Fighter* by Bruce Robertson, the most comprehensive work on this aspect of the aircraft.

Until the end of 1942 all Royal Air Force aircraft mark numbers were given in Roman numerals. From 1943 until 1948 the new aircraft entering service carried Arabic numbers while the older types continued to use Roman numerals. From 1948 all aircraft carried Arabic mark numbers. As a convention in this book, Spitfire marks up to the XVI are given in Roman numerals and those of later versions are given in Arabic numerals.

First published in 1977 by
Macdonald and Jane's Publishers Limited
Paulton House, 8 Shepherdess Walk,
London N1-7LW

Second impression 1978

ISBN 0 354 01077 8

Text design by Mike Jarvis

Printed in Great Britain by
NETHERWOOD DALTON & CO. LTD.,
Huddersfield

Contents

For Angela

Introduction

Probably no single aircraft in the history of aviation has had more written about it than the Spitfire. This is understandable: Reginald Mitchell's small, beautifully shaped fighter served its country well in an hour of need and became a symbol of defiance at a time when the British people saw their nation in mortal danger.

Over the years several people have written accounts of the evolution of the Spitfire. A close look at those covering the story of the aircraft up to the first flight of the prototype will, however, reveal quite major differences, leaving unanswered questions on matters of importance. Did an Air Ministry specification in fact restrict the design of the Type 224, the unsuccessful fighter designed by Mitchell which later evolved into the Spitfire? Which Air Ministry specifications influenced the design of the fighter? Indeed, were the Air Ministry specifications relevant to the Spitfire story at all, or was the whole project a private venture offered to the government after the aircraft had taken shape? The previously published accounts either do not attempt to answer these questions or, if they do give anwers, those answers are wrong. One will find all sorts of statements attributed to the all-important F. 7/30 and F.37/34 specifications, which bear no relation to their actual contents; errors have been repeated so many times that they have come to be treated as facts.

The purpose of the first part of this book, "The Road to the Spitfire", is to set straight the record on how the Spitfire evolved from Reginald Mitchell's original thoughts on a high-speed fighter late in 1931, until the first prototype flew in the spring of 1936. The first rule for a historian endeavouring to make an accurate reconstruction of a train of events is to refer, wherever possible, to authoritative documents written at the time or shortly afterwards. This I have done and the more important documents relating to the story are either quoted in part in the text of Chapter 1, or else reproduced in full in the Appendices which follow.

The second part of the book, "The Spitfire in Service", contains descriptions of some little-known incidents in the Spitfire's service career which enable it to be seen in a new light. Readers may find it of interest to learn that Reginald Mitchell's little fighter engaged enemy aircraft at altitudes up to 44,000 feet, undertook delivery flights over a distance equal to that from London to Leningrad and sank at least one German submarine; modified for the reconnaissance role, the aircraft remained effective and served in the front line into the 1950s. This book will shatter some long-held myths about the Spitfire, but it will also add to the already lustrous reputation of this aircraft.

In collecting the necessary information and documentary evidence for this book I have been fortunate in receiving help from many good friends. Amongst those who assisted were Charles Andrews, Beverley Shenstone, the late Air Marshal Sir Ralph Sorely, Air Vice-Marshal Michael Le Bas, Prince Emanuel Galitzine, Horst Goetz, Erich Sommer, Bill Marshall, Mr D. McCarthy and Chris Shores. Amongst those who kindly let me borrow photographs, many of them never previously published, were Beverley Shenstone, Keith Sissons, Dr Gordon Mitchell, Charles Andrews, Maurice Allward, Flight Lieutenant David Carroll, the late Bob Jones, Diether Lukesch, Group Captain M. Stephens, Horst Goetz, Paul Salkeld, Jerzy Cynk, Hugh Murland, Harry Van der Meer, John Rawlings, Franz Selinger and Bruce Rigelsford. I am grateful to the Royal Air Force Museum, the Air Historical Branch of the Ministry of Defence and the Public Record Office, for permission to reproduce passages from the documents held by them.

Alfred Price
Uppingham, Rutland

THE ROAD TO THE SPITFIRE

1.

SPECIFICATIONS AND SUBMISSIONS

The beautifully-proportioned Supermarine S.6B, which captured both the Schneider Trophy and the World Absolute Speed Record in 1931, marked the triumphant climax of Reginald Mitchell's efforts to perfect the design of the racing seaplane. Mitchell was to apply the knowledge in high speed aerodynamics thus gained to his fighter designs. *The Times*

The year 1931 saw the Supermarine Aircraft Company firmly established as world-leader in the design and production of high-speed racing seaplanes. At mid-day on September 13th Flight Lieutenant J. N. Boothman in an S.6B won the Schneider Trophy outright for his country by flying round the circular Spithead course at an average speed of 340.08 mph. In the afternoon Flight Lieutenant G. H. Stainforth, flying a sister aircraft, raised the world's absolute speed record to 379.05 mph; just over two weeks later, flying the Schneider Trophy winner fitted with a slightly modified Rolls-Royce R 27 engine, he raised his own record to 407.5 mph.

To have achieved any one of these things in a single year would have been a magnificent feat for any company. To do all three was a triumph for Supermarine's chief designer, Reginald Mitchell, and his team. After all of this, what followed could only be an anti-climax. During his work on entrants for the Schneider Trophy Mitchell had amassed a wealth of experience in the design of racing seaplanes. Yet in the nature of things, the market for such aircraft was extremely limited. The Company's main effort was devoted to the production of flying boats of various sizes; the hard-won knowledge of high speed flight could have little application for these.

This, then, was the state of affairs in the autumn of 1931 when the Air Ministry issued Specification F.7/30 for a fighter to replace the Bristol Bulldog in the Royal Air Force squadrons. The specification was approved by Air Commodore H. M. Cave-Brown-Cave, the Director of Technical Development at the Air Ministry, on October 1st; this document is reproduced in full as Appendix A. In the light of what has been said about it by writers since then, it is important to the Spitfire story not so much for what it said as for what it *did not* say.

As was usually the case, the specification document laid down the requirements for the new aircraft rather than its technical features; the latter were mentioned only in so far as they affected the operational use of the aircraft, for example the armament and the equipment to be carried, and the flight safety features to be embodied.

The essential requirements of the specification were laid down in paragraph 1, namely that the aircraft should have:

i Highest possible rate of climb
ii Highest possible speed above 15,000 feet
iii Fighting view
iv Manoeuvrability
v Capability of easy and rapid production in quantity
vi Ease of maintainance

It was to be armed with four machine guns, either four Vickers or two Vickers and two Lewis guns, and provision had to be made to carry four 20 pound bombs.

Several accounts have stated that Specification

The less-than-palatial Technical Office at Supermarine's Woolston works where the weight, stress and performance calculations for the Schneider Trophy Seaplanes, the Type 224 and later the Spitfire were worked out. *Shenstone*

The Drawing Office at Woolston, where the various Supermarine designs took detailed shape. *Shenstone*

F.7/30 called for a fighter powered by the Rolls-Royce Goshawk engine. This was not so. Paragraph 2 (a) clearly stated "Any approved British engine may be used." On the other hand, in 1931 and 1932 the Goshawk was the highest-powered British in-line engine suitable for use in a fighter and it is hardly surprising that several designers chose it for their submissions.

Quite apart from mis-statements on points of detail, several writers have repeated the myth that Specification F.7/30 was in some way restrictive and prevented designers from using their talents to the full to produce a world-beating aircraft. Examination of the actual document will not reveal any restriction of consequence,

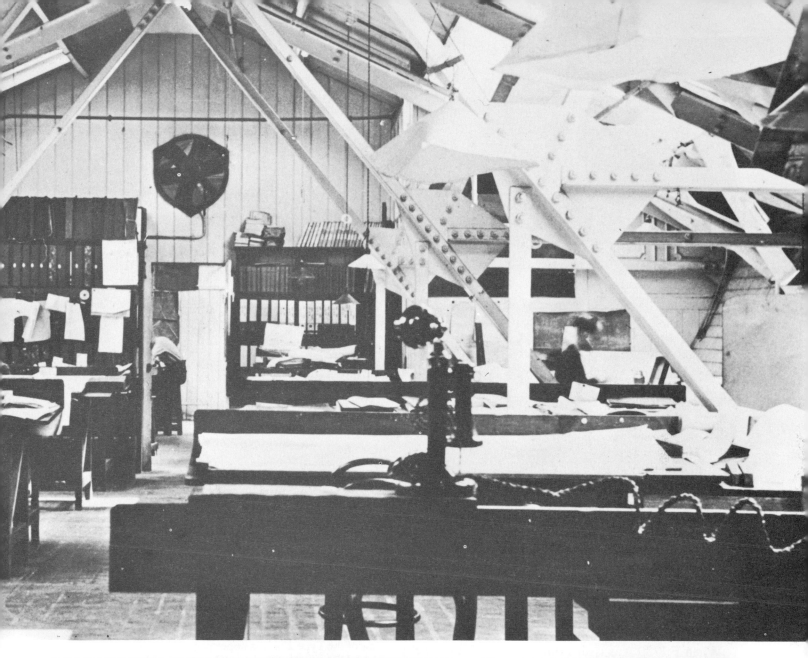

bearing in mind that the requirement was for a fighter aircraft for general service use. Designers were asked for a fighter giving the best possible rate-of-climb and speed and to achieve these they could use either a biplane or a monoplane configuration and any type of British engine.

When F.7/30 was issued times were difficult for the British aircraft industry, with the nation in the middle of a slump and orders hard to come by. As a result there was intense competition amongst aircraft companies to produce a fighter to win the design competition and thus secure what promised to be lucrative orders from the Royal Air Force and foreign governments. It was a measure of the latitude permitted by the Air Ministry specification that during the next three years no fewer than eight designs, with widely differing configurations, were built and submitted for consideration. Five of the submissions were biplanes: the Bristol 123, the Hawker PV 3, the Westland PV 4 and the Blackburn F.7/30 design, all of which were powered by the Goshawk, and the Gloster SS 37 powered by the Bristol Mercury radial. There were three monoplane designs: the Goshawk-powered Supermarine Type 224, the Mercury-powered Bristol Type 133 and the Jupiter-powered Vickers Jockey.

At that time the highest-powered engine available for use in fighters developed about 660 horse power, and on this nobody was going to go much faster than 250 mph.

The Supermarine Type 224 was Reginald Mitchell's submission for the 1931 Air Ministry F.7/30 Specification. *Above*: Overall view of the Type 224, with the cowling removed to reveal the evaporatively-cooled Goshawk engine; almost the whole of the leading edge of the wing was used as a condenser for the steam piped from the engine and the corrugated surface is clearly visible. *Opposite top*: Front view of the Type 224; the upper part of the wheel fairings housed the collector tanks for the coolant water after it had condensed from the steam. *Opposite centre*: Close-up of the nose of the Type 224, showing the ports for two of the four .303-in Vickers guns which were synchronised to fire through the airscrew; later the Supermarine Company would show that it could produce fighters with a much cleaner external surface. *Opposite bottom*: To reduce the drag due to interference between the air flowing over the wing and over the fuselage, later the Type 224 was fitted with wing fillets; the wool tufts enabled the direction of the airflow over the fillet to be observed in flight. *Shenstone*

At such a speed the advantage of the monoplane over the biplane configuration was by no means certain. Indeed the consensus amongst the leading British designers at the time was that the biplane was the better, as was shown by the greater proportion of biplanes entered for the F.7/30 competition. In the all-important matter of rate-of-climb a good biplane would usually beat a good monoplane and the former was considerably stronger and more manoeuvrable.

The Supermarine entry for the competition, the Type

224, was a low-winged monoplane with a fixed undercarriage. The design was accepted in August 1932 and the company received an Air Ministry contract to produce a single prototype. The 660 horse power Rolls-Royce Goshawk engine fitted to the aircraft employed evaporative cooling. When it was flowing through the water jacket round the engine, the coolant was water under pressure; as it left the engine the water was depressurised and the steam separated off. The water was then returned to the engine while the steam was piped through the condensers which ran almost the full length of the wing forward of the main spar. As it cooled the steam condensed into water, which trickled into collector tanks in the wheel fairings and was then pumped back to the engine. Although the condensers in the leading edge of the wing did produce drag, this was not so severe as that from a normal radiator. Moreover, evaporative cooling had the advantage over normal water cooling in that the engine could be run with the coolant temperature at just over 100°C without boiling taking place, which was more efficient from the thermodynamic point of view (the boiling point of unpressurised water at 15,000 feet is only 85°C).

The Supermarine Type 224 first flew in February 1934, to reveal an aircraft that did not perform impressively compared with some of its competitors. The fighter had a maximum speed of 238 mph and took eight minutes to climb to 15,000 feet. Moreover the

The winner of the F.7/30 fighter design competition was the Gloster SS 37, which went into production as the Gladiator. This aircraft demonstrated that on engines developing around 650 hp the monoplane configuration gave no clear advantage over the biplane for a fighter design. In horizontal flight the SS 37 was 4 mph faster than the Type 224, it could get to 15,000 feet $1\frac{1}{2}$ minutes earlier and it was a far more manoeuvrable and robust aircraft than the Supermarine design.

evaporative cooling system showed its drawbacks in this design as in others: during aerobatics or inverted flight water sometimes ran to where the steam should have been and steam floated to where the water should have been, resulting in a rapidly overheating engine.

The eventual winner of the F.7/30 competition was the Gloster SS 37, a radial-engined biplane which was to enter service in the Royal Air Force as the Gladiator. This aircraft was a refined version of the earlier Gauntlet; built as a private venture, it was a late entrant into the competition. The SS 37 had a maximum speed of 242 mph, which was faster than any of the competing monoplanes except for the Bristol 133. In rate-of-climb the Gloster fighter demonstrated the clear superiority of the biplane configuration in this respect: it reached

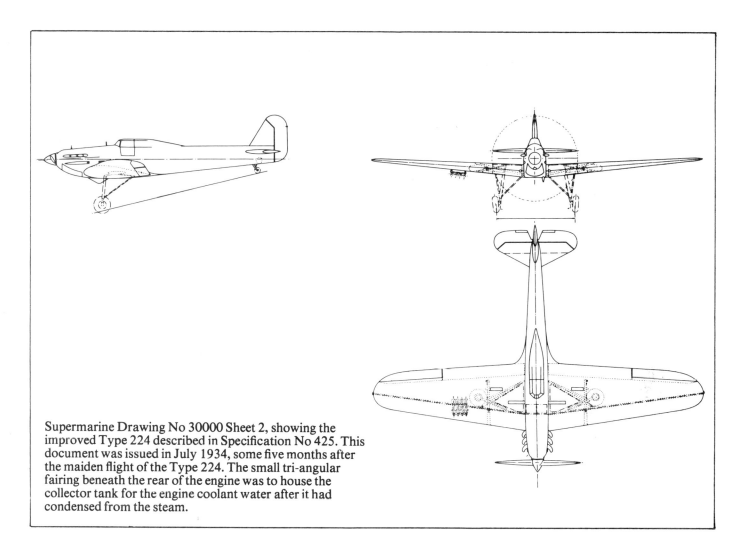

Supermarine Drawing No 30000 Sheet 2, showing the improved Type 224 described in Specification No 425. This document was issued in July 1934, some five months after the maiden flight of the Type 224. The small tri-angular fairing beneath the rear of the engine was to house the collector tank for the engine coolant water after it had condensed from the steam.

15,000 feet in $6\frac{1}{2}$ minutes (which was as fast as the first production Spitfire achieved during the service trials in 1938).

Some accounts have stated that it was the need for a large wing, to meet the F.7/30 requirement for a landing speed not exceeding 60 mph, that was a significant factor in the downfall of the Supermarine 224. This hardly squares with the fact that the landing speed of the first production Spitfire during its service trials was—60 mph.

For the reasons for the lack of success of the Supermarine Type 224, one must look away from the Air Ministry specification. The aircraft was Reginald Mitchell's first attempt at a landplane fighter design and many of the problems were new to him. He knew how to make an aircraft go fast; but achieving a good rate of climb, a good view for the pilot and reasonable manoeuvrability were things he had not had to achieve before. Also, as Beverley Shenstone states in his account *Shaping the Spitfire* which follows, Mitchell and his team did not feel that winning the F.7/30 competition would place any great demand on their abilities.

> "My own personal feeling is that the design team had done so well with the S.5 and S.6 series of racing floatplanes, which in the end reached speeds of over 400 mph, that they had thought it would be child's play to design a fighter intended to fly at little over half that speed. They never made that mistake again!"

The Supermarine design team was to show that it could do a great deal better.

During the summer of 1934 Mitchell and his team worked on the design of a cleaned-up derivative of the Type 224, the Type 300. Supermarine Specification No 425, outlining the proposal, was issued on July 16th 1934 and was submitted to the Air Ministry for consideration. Ten days later the document was followed by Specification No 425a, which described the same aircraft in slightly greater detail; the latter specification is reproduced in full as Appendix B. Essentially the proposed aircraft was a Type 224 fitted with an enclosed cockpit, a slightly smaller wing and a retractable undercarriage. With these improvements the

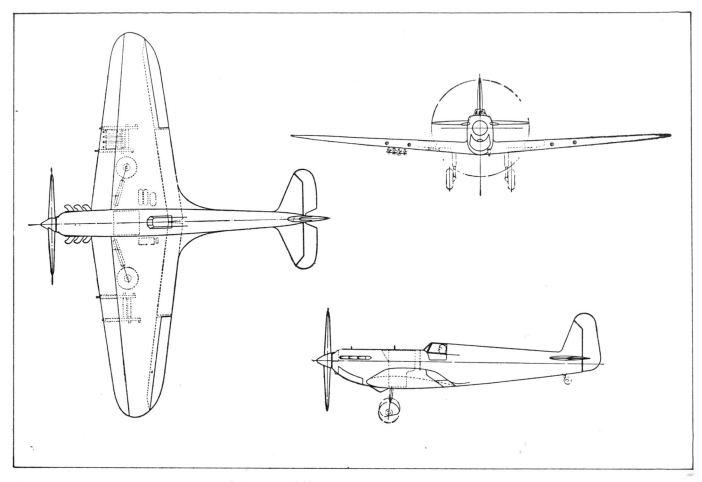

company estimated that the revised fighter would have a maximum speed about 30 mph greater than the Type 224, on a Goshawk engine of the same power.

The Air Ministry was lukewarm towards the new proposal, which offered a performance no better than designs from other firms bidding for the fighter contract. There was a suggestion that the new Supermarine fighter would do better if it was re-engined with the Napier Dagger, an air-cooled in-line engine which was then developing nearly 700 horse power with 800 horse power expected later. The Dagger did not find favour with the company, however, and at a board meeting at Vickers (Supermarine's parent company) on November 6th this was turned down; the directors were negotiating with Rolls-Royce for something better. At the same meeting Mitchell received permission to begin detailed design work on the Type 300 fighter, the lines of which had been further refined since the 425 Specification in July. The board decided that the fighter was to be built as a private venture, without waiting for a government contract.

Soon after Mitchell received permission to go ahead with the Type 300, it was agreed between Supermarine and Rolls-Royce that the fighter should be powered by the new PV XII engine (later named the Merlin). The decision to use the PV XII was the great turning point in the story of Reginald Mitchell's efforts to produce a

This project, depicted on Supermarine Drawing No 30000 Sheet 11, shows one of the final Type 224 derivatives powered by the Goshawk engine. Issued in the autumn of 1934, it shows an aircraft with a faired cockpit and a thin wing.

first-rate fighter aircraft. Before that time, the Type 224 and its design derivatives had been only mid-field runners in the race for fighter performance; with a maximum of only about 660 horse power from the engine previously available, speeds were limited to about 250 mph and little advantage could be gained from the subtleties of design Mitchell had learnt from the work on his high-speed seaplanes. The PV XII opened up entirely new prospects. Although it was suffering from teething troubles and was still far from ready for production, in July 1934 the engine had passed its 100 hour type test giving 625 horse power for take-off and 790 horse power at 12,000 feet; the target figure for power output was 1,000 horse power. Now Mitchell could see that speeds of well over 300 mph were in prospect, where streamlining would be all-important and he would be able to use his hard-won experience to good effect. The decision to combine the revised Type 300 airframe with the PV XII engine drew immediate Air Ministry interest in the project and on December 1st

Some of the men responsible for the Spitfire

Above, from left to right: Captain J. 'Mutt' Summers, who took the prototype on her maiden flight; Major Harold Payne, Assistant Chief Designer; Reginald Mitchell, the Chief Designer at Supermarine Aviation; Mr. S. Scott-Hall, the Air Ministry Resident Technical Officer; Jeffrey Quill, who later became the firm's Chief Test Pilot. *Dr G. Mitchell. Centre left:* Joseph Smith, the Chief Draughtsman during the design of the Spitfire, led the design team after Mitchell's death. *Centre right:* Alan Clifton, head of the Supermarine Technical Office. *Below (left)* Victor Bibire, *(centre)* Wilfred Hennessy and *(right)* Harold Holmes did stress calculations for the new fighter. *Shenstone*

1934 contract AM 361140/34 was issued, providing the sum of £10,000 for the construction of a prototype fighter to Mitchell's "improved F.7/30" design.

Several previous accounts have suggested that the Spitfire was throughout a private venture. This is not borne out by the documentary evidence. In fact the Type 300 with the PV XII engine was a private venture for less than a month, ending with the issue of the Air Ministry contract on December 1st. Whether a particular venture was private or government depended, essentially, on whose money was at risk: if the firm's capital was at stake it was a private venture; if the government put up the risk capital it was a government venture. The aircraft in Supermarine Specification No 425, and the early improvements to it, had indeed been drawn up at the company's expense; but the expense was not large and no constructional work had yet started on the new fighter.

The contract for the Supermarine Type 300 was formalised on January 3rd 1935 when the Deputy Director of Technical Development at the Air Ministry, Major J. S. Buchanan, put his signature to Specification F.37/34. This was in fact a short addendum to Specification F.7/30 and permitted little that the former did not; the Specification is reproduced as Appendix C. Contrary to what several accounts have stated, the specification did not mention any performance targets for the new fighter; and, as Paragraph 4 (d) makes clear, it called for an aircraft with four machine guns and not the eight that were later fitted. F.37/34 specified that the fighter was to be powered with the PV XII engine; paragraph 2 (d) stated that the engine was to be evaporatively cooled, as had been the Goshawk in the Type 224.

The overwhelming credit for the world-beating fighter which now began to take detailed shape in the drawing office at Woolston near Southampton must of course go to Reginald Mitchell and his small design team and to the Rolls-Royce engineers working to perfect the engine. But there were others, working in government departments, who deserve a share also.

As has been noted, Specification F.37/34 called for a fighter armed with four machine guns. It was becoming clear that these might not provide sufficient fire-power to destroy the fast monoplane bombers which were coming into service. The very speed of an interception would allow only a short firing pass; and far more hits were necessary to inflict lethal damage on all-metal structure than on an older fabric-covered aircraft. Since the beginning of 1933 Squadron Leader Ralph Sorley had been in charge of the Operational Requirements section at the Air Ministry; he later wrote:

"Like so many others, I had spent many years trying to hit targets with one, two or even four machine-guns with, I confess, singularly poor results. Others were so much better but I estimated that, if one could hold the sight on for longer than two seconds, that was better than average.

We were now going to have to hold it on at appreciably higher speeds so the average might even be less than two seconds. The two or four-gunned biplanes had been equipped with Vickers guns in general, the residue of vast stocks left over from the 1914–18 War. By 1934 a new Browning gun was at last being tested in Britain which offered a higher rate of fire. After much arithmetic and burning of midnight oil, I reached the answer of eight guns as being the number required to give a lethal dose in two seconds of fire. I reckoned that the bomber's speed would probably be such as to allow the pursuing fighter only one chance of attack, so it must be destroyed in that vital two-second burst."

Sorley's arguments convinced the Deputy Chief of the Air Staff, Air Vice Marshal Edgar Ludlow-Hewitt, and as a result the main 1934 fighter specification, F.5/34, called for an aircraft armed with eight machine guns. This specification has often been linked with the aircraft which later became the Spitfire, but in fact there was no formal link between the two.

The specification which *did* affect the armament of the new Supermarine fighter was F.10/35, which appeared in the spring of 1935 and reflected the latest Air Ministry thinking as regards fighters; the Specification is reproduced as Appendix D. This asked for a fighter with "Not less than 6 guns, but 8 guns are desirable." Paragraph 3 contained the intriguing statement:

"It is contemplated that some or all of these guns should be mounted to permit of a degree of elevation and traverse with some form of control from the pilot's seat. Though it is not at present possible to give details, it is desirable that designers should be aware of the possibility of this development, which should not, however, be allowed to delay matters at this stage."

The author discussed the armament of the Spitfire with Sir Ralph Sorley (as he later became) in October 1974, shortly before he died. He made it clear that in 1935 it was far from certain that the average squadron pilot, flying a monoplane with a wing loading far higher than that of any of the fighters then in use, would be able to hold his sights on a bomber for the two seconds necessary to deliver the lethal burst. Hence the suggestion of semi-movable guns, which in the event came to nothing.

Towards the end of April Sorley visited the Supermarine works to discuss the new fighter with Mitchell and on May 1st he informed the new Deputy Chief of the Air Staff, Air Vice-Marshal Christopher Courtney:

"On Friday, 26th April, 1935, I saw at Supermarines a mock-up of a fighter which they are building to Specification 37/34. This is one got out by A.M.R.D. [the Air Member for Research and Development—Air Marshal Sir Hugh Dowding] to cover the redesign of the Supermarine F.7/30.

2. According to the 37/34 Specification it is to comply

generally with the requirements of the F.7/30 Specification subject to certain concessions. As designed, it has every feature required by our latest specification 10/35 with the following differences:

	37/34	10/35
(i) Guns	4 in wings	6 or 8 in wings
(ii) Bombs	4 × 20	Nil
(iii) Fuel	94 gallons	66 gallons
	$= \frac{1}{2}$ hr maximum	$= \frac{1}{4}$ hr maximum
	plus nearly 2 hrs	plus 1 hr at
	at normal rpm	normal rpm

3. Mitchell received the Air Staff requirements for the 10/35 while I was there and is naturally desirous of bringing the aircraft now building into line with this specification. He says he can include 4 additional guns without trouble or delay. (ii) and (iii) are, of course, deletions which he welcomes. The saving in fuel amounts to 273 lbs (Mitchell's estimate is 59 gallons); thus there is a big saving in weight (180 lb even after adding the additional 4 guns).

4. [In this paragraph Sorley referred to the new Hawker fighter, which later became the Hurricane.]

5. Both aircraft look to be excellent in the hands of Mitchell and Camm and I suggest that they are likely to be successes. I say this because I foresee in these two aircraft the equipment we should aim at obtaining for new squadrons and re-equipping Bulldog squadrons in 1936 *if* we commence action *now* to make this possible."

Top: Believed to be the only one to survive of the wooden mock-up of the F.37/34 this photograph was taken in 1936 in the Supermarine hangar at Hythe where Stranraer flying boats were being assembled. The mock-up, less wings, had been hoisted out of the way prior to disposal; note the transport joint mid-way along the fuselage. *via C.F. Andrews*

Above: Squadron Leader Ralph Sorley pressed for the new Supermarine fighter to be fitted with the eight-gun armament. *IWM*

Sorley then went on to suggest that either or both of the new monoplane fighters should be placed into production without waiting for the results of flight trials, even at the expense of the Gloster F.7/30 (which later became the Gladiator): "I am aware that this is an unorthodox method but with the political situation as it is and the possibility of increased expansion close upon us we should take steps to produce the latest design in the shortest possible time."

At this time Sorley was only a Squadron Leader; his position in charge of Operational Requirements meant that he had access to officers on the Air Staff, but he had very little power of his own. He could achieve his aims only by convincing those who held real power within the Service.

On May 5th Air Commodore R. H. Verney, the Director of Technical Development, commented on Sorley's letter:

"1. As a matter of principle I am against asking firms to make alterations on prototypes once the decision to place the order has been given, and I have had my design conference with the designer. But I realise that there are special circumstances which may make the cases of these monoplanes an exception to the rule.
2. As regards the Supermarine F.37/34 I agree that there should be no great difficulty in adding the four additional guns. Deleting the bombs would be a help, but I should not be in favour of reducing the tankage, as this could be done in production models if required; it is always much easier to decrease than to increase, and experience shews that as the engine power goes up we often wish to add extra tankage. Nor need the aeroplanes be flown with full tanks.
3. [This paragraph dealt with the Hawker monoplane fighter.]
4. We must realise that we have very little experience of monoplanes of this type, and difficulties in developing them are certain to have to be faced. I should be very opposed to holding back on the Gloster F.7/30 with Perseus engine, and feel that we should press this forward as quickly as possible, as a reserve.
5. The question as to how much should be risked to save delay in putting either or both of these two monoplanes into production, if they should prove satisfactory, is a matter of policy rather beyond me. It should be realised that if the design and construction of jigs, etc, were begun there would be a risk of serious alteration, and possibly wholesale scrapping, if changes have to be made. I would rather say that directly the aeroplanes have been flown and we know the best or the worst, as the case may be, that then would be the time for a production gamble if circumstances necessitate.

In his covering minute to Verney's letter, Air Marshal Dowding told Air Vice-Marshal Courtney:

"DTD's comments are at Enc 4A. I agree generally with them. I think we should adopt *the principle* of leaving the tankage unaltered, as the fuselage and wing shapes and

Air Marshal Hugh Dowding was Air Member for Research and Development on the Air Council from 1930 to 1936, and held ultimate responsibility for the aircraft specifications issued by the Air Ministry including those leading up to the Spitfire. Later he was to command Royal Air Force Fighter Command during the critical Battle of Britain period, when the Spitfire made its mark on history. Thus, more than any other air commander before or since, Dowding had a direct influence on the shaping of the weapons his force was to use in action. *IWM*

dimensions are already irrevocably settled. We need not fill the tanks always and, as DTD says, it is easier to cut down than to increase. We may *have* to cut down the wing tankage [in the Hawker fighter] to fit in the guns. I think the custom of ordering jigs and tools for more than two types should be referred to A.M.S.O. [the Air Member for Supply and Organisation, Air Chief Marshal Sir Cyril Newall]. Personally I think DTD's suggestion (to wait until the machines have taken the air) is sound."

Towards the end of May, following discussions with the Chief of the Air Staff (Air Chief Marshal Sir Edward Ellington), in a letter to Dowding Air Vice-Marshal Courtney delivered the final edict from his department on the changes required by the Service to the new Supermarine and Hawker fighters:

"In the first place I quite agree that nothing should be allowed to delay the construction and flying tests of these aeroplanes. But I think we could possibly bring these aircraft into line with the F.10/35 Specification without necessarily imposing delays.

2. Guns

As regards the Supermarine, since DTD says there should be no great difficulty in adding the four additional guns, I should certainly like this done. [Then he went on to discuss the new Hawker fighter].

3. Bombs

I imagine that the deletion of the bomb requirement from the specification will please everyone and should make things easier for the firms.

4. Petrol

I agree with you that the tankage should be left unaltered, unless it has to be cut down in order to fit in the extra guns.

5. Jigging and Tooling

I raised the question with the C.A.S. recently and the ruling was that no steps should be taken in this direction until the aircraft had actually been flight tested."

It remained only to tie up the contractual side of the business and on May 28th Air Commodore Verney wrote to the Air Ministry Director of Contracts, Mr. B. E. Holloway:

"In Minute 7 of S.35617 A.M.R.D. [Dowding] has agreed to the Air Staff proposals that this aeroplane should be brought into line with the F.10/35 Specification as soon as possible. This involves:

(a) The design and manufacture of a new set of wings to take 8 Vickers Mark V or Browning guns with 300 rounds of ammunition per gun . . .

(b) Reduction of the fuel to 75 gallons, though the actual tankage need not be reduced unless it is necessary to do so to provide space for the guns.

(c) Deletion of the bomb requirements.

Could you please ask the firm to quote for the above as an addition to the contract, but at the same time inform them that it is not desired that any alteration should be made to the aeroplane at the present state of manufacture, as it is of the utmost importance that it should be completed and flying as quickly as possible. It is desired that the design and manufacture of new wings should proceed at the same time, so the conversion could be made at a later stage in the flying trials."

So much for the background to the fitting of the eight machine guns into the new fighter. A further change, introduced into the design at about the same time, was equally important though less spectacular. One area of weakness in the initial design of the Type 300, as in its predecessor, was the method of cooling the engine. The

Working at the Royal Aircraft Establishment at Farnborough, Mr F.W. Meredith pioneered the development of ducted radiator cooling which was to make it possible for Mitchell to dispense with the unpredictable evaporative cooling for his new fighter.

evaporative system, with its uneven operation and general vulnerability to battle damage, was hardly suitable for a combat aircraft. Could anything better be done, without having to resort to the draggy radiators that Mitchell had tried so hard to avoid in his high-speed designs? In retrospect the problem of engine cooling might seem only a trivial part of the story, but we have seen that it could contribute to the downfall of a fighter.

When an early version of the Merlin was running at full power, the cooling system had to remove and dissipate 11,500 CHUs (centigrade heat units) of heat per minute; this is roughly the equivalent of 370 one-kilowatt electric fires running simultaneously! The engine oil carried away a further 930 CHUs per minute, the equivalent of 30 one-kilowatt fires. Unless all of this heat was conducted away, the engine would grind to a steaming halt.

The solution to the cooling problem came from the Royal Aircraft Establishment at Farnborough, where Mr F. W. Meredith had been experimenting with a new type of ducted radiator. In the ducted radiator the air entered from the front, via a duct whose cross-sectional area was progressively widened to reduce the velocity and therefore increase the pressure of the air; the air then passed through the matrix of the radiator where it was heated and expanded; then it accelerated as it passed through the divergent duct at the rear. In other words, the ducted radiator acted rather like the present-day ram jet: the ram air was compressed, heated, and then expelled from the rear with increased velocity to produce thrust. The amount of thrust produced from the ducted radiator was small and only under optimum conditions did it exceed the drag. But previous types of radiator had all been major drag-producing items, so Meredith's work represented an important step forward.

Meredith issued a paper on his findings in June 1935; the ducted radiator was thankfully received at Supermarine and faithfully applied to the new fighter.

There remained the problem of getting the Merlin to run at its most efficient temperature at high altitude, without the unpressurised coolant boiling. Rolls-Royce engineers solved this problem by using as the coolant almost pure ethylene glycol, which boiled at 160°C at sea level and 120°C at 27,000 feet. Now it was possible to get the engine to run at a more efficient temperature, hot enough for efficient combustion but not so hot as to raise mechanical problems, with little or no drag from the cooling system.

By the summer of 1935 the Spitfire design existed in all of its important aspects. Since the Supermarine 425

proposal of the previous summer, its shape had changed out of all recognition: the new fighter had a much thinner, elliptically-shaped wing; it was powered by a Merlin engine with ducted radiator cooling; and it was to carry an eight-gun armament.

Perhaps surprisingly, in view of the undoubted aerodynamic efficiency of its design, very little wind tunnel work was done for the Spitfire. As Beverley Shenstone says in his account, at that time wind tunnels were not efficient and tended to give misleading results. By making step-by-step improvements to the Type 224 the Supermarine design team knew they must produce a better aircraft. Indeed, the only wind tunnel tests conducted for the new fighter were those in the 7 ft tunnel at Farnborough in November 1935, using a quarter-scale model of the starboard half of the aircraft to determine the optimum shape of the ducted radiator.

During the autumn of 1935 the new fighter, referred to usually as the F.37/34, began to take shape in a restricted area in one of the erecting shops at Supermarine's Woolston plant. After a visit to the works to

The only wind tunnel tests conducted with the Supermarine F.37/34 prior to the maiden flight were those in the 7-foot tunnel at Farnborough in November 1935, to determine the optimum shape for the ducted radiator. As this drawing made at the time shows, for the tests a $\frac{1}{4}$ scale model of the starboard half of the aircraft was mounted upside-down in the tunnel.

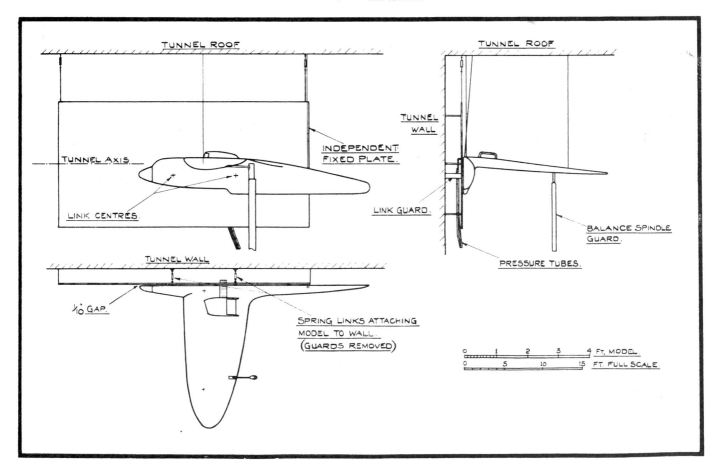

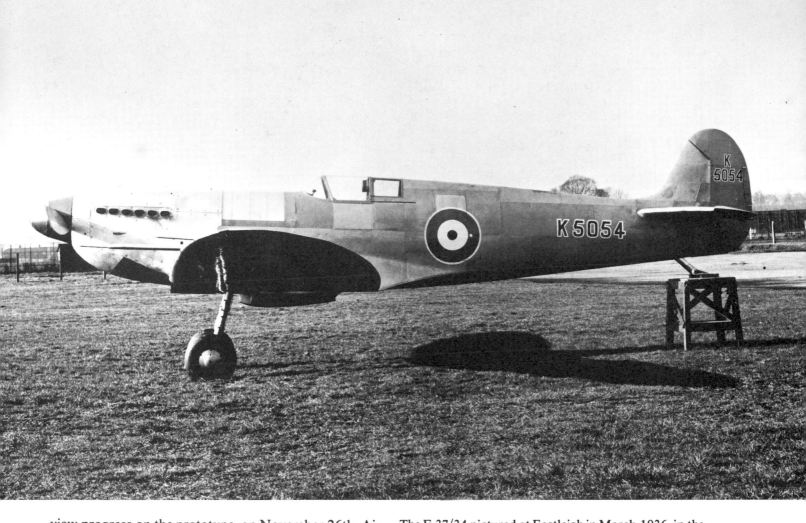

view progress on the prototype, on November 26th, Air Commodore Verney wrote:

"1. The fuselage is nearly completed, and the engine installed. The wings are being plated, and some parts of the undercarriage still have to be finished. I like the simple design of the undercarriage very much. Also the flush riveting of the surfaces of the fuselage and wings. The glycol radiator is in the starboard wing, with controlled inlet cooling. Tubular honeycomb oil coolers (of American manufacture) are set forward under the engine.
2. As far as I can see it cannot be flying this year, but it should be early in January. It is in many ways a much more advanced design than the Hawker, and should be a great deal lighter."

In the event the work took a little longer than Verney had thought: the prototype was not finished until February 1936 and it took the air for the first time on March 6th with Captain J. 'Mutt' Summers at the controls.

The initial performance report on the fighter, which now carried the name "Spitfire", was issued in July 1936 (Air Ministry Report No M/629 Int 1). Compiled after tests at the Aeroplane and Armament Experimental Establishment at Martlesham Heath the document showed the aircraft's performance to be as follows: maximum speed 349 mph at 16,800 feet and 324 mph at 30,000 feet; climb to 15,000 feet in 5 minutes 42

The F.37/34 pictured at Eastleigh in March 1936, in the form in which she made her maiden flight. At this time the aircraft was unpainted and lacked fairings on the undercarriage legs. *Crown Copyright.*

seconds, to 20,000 feet in 8 minutes 12 seconds and to 30,000 feet in 17 minutes. The service ceiling (the altitude at which the rate of climb fell to below 100 feet per minute) was 35,400 feet. During these trials the aircraft weighed 5,332 pounds, with ballast in place of the guns and ammunition. The only change in the external appearance of the aircraft, following its maiden flight, had been a reduction in the area of the rudder aerodynamic balance.

The July report was followed by a second in September entitled "Handling Trials of the Spitfire K 5054"; this document is reproduced as Appendix E. It revealed two complaints with the aircraft. The first was that the service test pilots found that there was too much 'float' during the landing approach and they felt the effect of the flaps would be enhanced if their angle in the lowered position were increased from 60° to 90°; on production aircraft the flap system was altered so that they could be lowered to 90°. The second complaint was that the cockpit canopy was found to be very difficult to open at speeds of over 300 mph; this would be overcome on

Above: Command Performance. 'Bulled-up' for the occasion, the prototype is seen being inspected by King Edward VIII at Martlesham Heath in July 1936. *Charles Brown*

Below: With a more workaday appearance, the prototype is seen during her early trials at Eastleigh. To the right, in the background, may be seen Reginald Mitchell's Rolls Royce car.

Opposite page: The prototype pictured in the hangar at Eastleigh in April 1936, soon after painting. *Shenstone*

Two views of the prototype late in 1936, following the fitting of the armament and a manifold over the exhausts. Note the smoothness of the skinning of the nose, compared with that of the Type 224 shown in the earlier photograph. *Shenstone*

production aircraft by the fitting of a small push-out panel on the port side of the perspex hood which could be knocked out by the pilot's elbow, to equalise the pressure inside and outside the canopy and thus make it easier to open.

In June 1936, even before the reports on the Spitfire's performance and handling characteristics were complete, the Air Ministry felt confident enough with the aircraft to place an order for 310. Specification F.16/36 covered the modifications required on the production aircraft as well as giving the mass of "nitty gritty" detail necessary for a service contract. The required changes to the prototype were given in Paragraph 10, which is reproduced as Appendix F.

The year 1937 saw a steady deterioration in Reginald Mitchell's health. An operation in March to arrest his cancer proved unsuccessful and his condition was found to be incurable. He died in June.

A few months after Mitchell's death his great legacy to the nation, the prototype Spitfire, appeared in fighting trim. Modified where possible to conform with F.16/36, it carried a radio and bore a coat of camouflage paint. It was re-engined with a Merlin II developing a maximum of 1,030 horse power, 40 horse power more than the Merlin C which had powered the aircraft during its early flights.

One interesting development fitted to the Spitfire at this time was the ejector exhaust system, developed for the Merlin by Messrs R. N. Dorey and H. Pearson at Rolls-Royce. Each minute that it ran at full power, the Merlin II gulped in through the carburettor air intake a volume of air about as great as a single-decker bus; after combustion, this air was squirted out of the exhausts at about 1,300 mph. By carefully canting the exhaust pipes rearwards, the Rolls-Royce engineers found that they could get 70 pounds of thrust—the equivalent of 70 horse power at 300 mph—almost for nothing. It was a useful addition and, with the extra power from the new engine, would increase the speed of the prototype to about 360 mph.

This, then, was the road to the Spitfire, the winding path followed by Reginald Mitchell and his team to produce their world-beating fighter. Their first attempt, the Supermarine Type 224, had not been a success because its designers had not grasped the problems involved in producing a fighter. The Supermarine 425 proposal offered a fighter that was a bit better and which, with further improvements by Mitchell and powered by the engine that was to become the Merlin, was ordered by the Air Ministry under Specification F.37/34. As the fighter was being re-designed to take the heavier new engine, the parallel-tapered wing gave way to the beautiful elliptical shape which was to characterise the Spitfire for most of its life. In the spring of 1935 the Air Ministry issued its new fighter specification F.10/35, which called for a fighter with six or pre-ferably eight machine guns. Mitchell was quick to grasp the need for an increase in fire-power over the four guns which were to have armed his fighter, and offered to redesign it to conform with the new requirement. Fortunately, with a bit of juggling, the fighter's thin elliptical wing could be altered to accommodate the eight guns and their ammunition boxes. Next, in about the middle of 1935, the evaporative cooling system planned for the engine gave way to the altogether more satisfactory ducted radiator system pioneered by engineers at Farnborough. This was the final major change to the fighter, which was then built and made its first flight in March 1936. Three months later, after successful initial flight trials, the Air Ministry placed an order for 310 similar aircraft modified to conform with Specification F.16/36.

Thus described, the story of the road leading to the Spitfire may seem simple enough; but the path is easy to follow only to those who have to hand the documents that chart the route. To the others there are pitfalls at almost every corner.

One major point of error in several previous accounts is the notion that the Spitfire was a private venture. It certainly began that way, but very early on the company was pleased to surrender private independence for government cash. From December 1934 the project was a government venture. Jeffrey Quill, who was Chief Test Pilot at Supermarines throughout almost the entire development life of the Spitfire and is one of the authorities on this aircraft, was to write (letter in *Flight* March 15th 1973):

"From time to time attempts have been made to suggest that the Spitfire was a private venture produced in the face of opposition from an obtuse and obstructionist Air Staff... [This] has no foundation in fact.

In 1934, when the final design of the Spitfire was completed, there existed a very close personal relationship between the designers in industry, the Air Staff and the Government establishments. Air Ministry specifications therefore had the benefit of important inputs from the great designers and from the establishments. Arguments and disagreements there may sometimes have been, but this was part of the process and was just as it should have been. In fact very much the same situation exists today albeit in a more formal and complex way.

The Spitfire was a great national achievement and credit for its outstanding success must be spread over a wide area of effort both inside and outside the industry which produced it. Attempts to suggest otherwise are both misleading and unseemly."

The prototype Spitfire had cost the British taxpayer £15,776; rarely has government money been better spent.

2

SHAPING THE SPITFIRE

by Beverley Shenstone MASc, Hon FRAeS, FAIA

Few people can be better qualified to speak about the design of the Spitfire than Beverley Shenstone, who served as an aerodynamicist in Reginald Mitchell's team when the fighter was conceived. In this account he gives a fascinating insight into the thinking behind some of the features incorporated in the aircraft.

In 1929, at the age of 23, I received my second, Master's, degree in aeronautical engineering from the University of Toronto. At that time there was very little aircraft manufacture or design in Canada, so to continue in my chosen profession I had to move abroad. First I went to Germany, where I was allowed to work for almost no pay at the Junkers Works at Dessau. I was employed in the sheet-metal and other shops, where the main production effort was directed towards the Junkers 34, a single-engined all-metal eight seater transport.

In the summer of 1930 I took a month's leave to go to the Wasserkuppe gliding centre, where I met Alexander Lippisch who was later to do a lot of work on delta wings. We became firm friends and with his help I wrote a couple of papers on the design of wings for long-range aircraft. I also won my 'C' gliding certificate.

Early in 1931 I moved to England, to try for a job with one of the aircraft firms and further improve my working knowledge of aviation. The first firm I went to was Hawker, where I was interviewed by Sydney Camm. He said to me: "If there's a specification for a single-seat fighter and you are asked to draw up a design, what is the first thing you would do?" I told him I should first decide whether to make it a biplane or a monoplane. He replied: "No you wouldn't. It would be a biplane!" Obviously my ideas did not fit in with those Camm thought an aerodynamicist ought to have at that time. I did not get the job.

Beverley Shenstone, pictured shortly before he took up his post as an aerodynamicist on Reginald Mitchell's design team. *Shenstone*

After a couple more tries I went to Supermarine at Southampton, where Reginald Mitchell saw me. He asked about my previous experience, so I told him about the work I had done in Germany and the papers I had written about wings for long-range aircraft. He told me that his design department was working on the plans for a six-engined monoplane flying boat for the Royal Air Force. He sent for the drawing of the wing and asked me what I thought of the design. I took a good nervous look at it and then told him that, on the basis of my previous work, I thought it would be better with a bit more taper; it would then be lighter and, with a bit of care in the shaping, probably just as effective. From the look on his face I could see that he was taken aback by my comments; he asked me to leave a contacting address and said he could call me if he needed me.

After a short delay I received a letter offering me a post as an aerodynamicist with Supermarine. I went back to see Mitchell and he said: "I've been thinking about what you said about the wing of the flying boat. See if you really can do it for less weight than the present design." I was given three months to prove myself; if I was successful there would be a permanent post open to me at the princely salary of £500 per year. In the event the six-engined flying boat was never built, but Mitchell was sufficiently impressed with my work on the wing to confirm my post with his design team.

When I joined Supermarine the design of the Type 224 fighter was virtually complete and I had little to do with it. As is now well known, that fighter was not successful. My own personal feeling is that the design team had done so well with the S.5 and S.6 series of racing floatplanes, which in the end reached speeds of over 400 mph, that they had thought it would be child's play to design a fighter intended to fly at little over half that speed. They never made that mistake again!

The flight tests of the Type 224, carried out during the early part of 1934, revealed that it had only a mediocre performance. The members of the design team had had considerable experience with high-speed aircraft, however, and it did not take long to pin-point the causes. The fighter's wing was thicker than it need have been, the leading edge housing the steam condenser was corrugated, the undercarriage was fixed and the cockpit was open; there was far more drag than was strictly necessary. Even on the 660 horse power from a Goshawk engine, we knew we could improve on the 238 mph maximum speed of the Type 224.

In the middle of 1934 the company submitted a proposal to the Air Ministry for an improved fighter based on the Type 224, the Type 300. By cleaning up the wing, fitting a retractable undercarriage and enclosing the cockpit we planned to reduce the drag. Moreover, by the use of split trailing-edge flaps we sought to achieve the same landing speed with a wing 14 per cent smaller in area. Overall, we calculated that these improvements would raise the maximum speed by about 30 mph, for no increase in engine power.

Still the Air Ministry was lukewarm towards our proposal: the advance in performance over competing fighter types was not great enough. Then, late in 1934, the company decided to re-engine the fighter with the new Rolls-Royce PV XII engine, later named the Merlin. This engine was being developed to give a target output of 1,000 horse power and the decision to use it was an important milestone on the road leading up to the Spitfire. On this power our fighter would exceed 300 mph by a wide margin and Air Ministry interest was immediate. In December the company received a contract to build a prototype and the following month Specification F.37/34 was issued, written round our revised Type 300 design.

Spurred by the government contract, we began the detailed design of the new fighter. The elliptical wing was decided upon quite early on. Aerodynamically it was the best for our purpose because the induced drag, that caused in producing lift, was lowest when this shape was used; the ellipse was an ideal shape, theoretically a perfection. There were other advantages, so far as we were concerned. To reduce drag we wanted the lowest possible wing thickness-to-chord ratio, consistent with the necessary strength. But near the root the wing had to be thick enough to accommodate the retracted undercarriage and the guns; so to achieve a good thickness-to-chord ratio we wanted the wing to have a wide chord near the root. A straight-tapered wing starts to reduce in chord from the moment it leaves the root; an elliptical wing, on the other hand, tapers only very slowly at first then progressively more rapidly towards

the tip. Mitchell was an intensely practical man and he liked practical solutions to problems. I remember once discussing the wing shape with him and he commented: "I don't give a b.... whether it's elliptical or not, so long as it covers the guns!" The ellipse was simply the shape which allowed us the thinnest possible wing with sufficient room inside to carry the necessary structure and the things we wanted to cram in. And it looked nice.

The Type 224 had had a thick wing section and we wanted to improve on that. The NACA 2200 series aerofoil section was just right and we varied the thickness-to-chord ratio to fit our own requirements: we ended up with 13 per cent of the chord at the root and 6

per cent at the tip, the thinnest we thought we could get away with. Joe Smith, in charge of structural design, deserves all credit for producing a wing that was both strong enough and stiff enough within the severe volumetric constraints.

It has been suggested that we at Supermarine had cribbed the Spitfire's elliptical wing shape from that of the German Heinkel 70 transport. This was not so. The elliptical wing shape had been used in other aircraft and its advantages were well known. Our wing was much thinner than that of the Heinkel and had a quite different section. In any case it would have been simply asking for trouble to have copied a wing shape from an aircraft

Professor Ernst Heinkel, right, pictured with the Heinkel 70 transport whose clean exterior made such an impression on Shenstone. *via Schliephake*

designed for an entirely different purpose.

The Heinkel 70 did have an influence on the Spitfire, but in a rather different way. I had seen the German aircraft at the Paris Aero Show and been greatly impressed by the smoothness of its skin. There was not a rivet head to be seen. I ran my hand over the surface and it was so smooth that I thought it might be constructed of wood. I was so impressed that I wrote to Ernst Heinkel, without Mitchell's knowledge, and asked how he had done it;

was the aircraft skin made of metal or wood? I received a very nice letter back from the German firm, saying that the skinning was of metal with the rivets countersunk and very carefully filled before the application of several layers of paint. When we got down to the detailed design of the F.37/34 I referred to the Heinkel 70 quite a lot during our discussions. I used it as a criterion for aerodynamic smoothness and said that if the Germans could do it so, with a little more effort, could we. Of course, the Heinkel's several layers of paint added greatly to the weight; we had to do the best we could without resorting to that.

One point which some may find surprising is that we made hardly any use of wind tunnel testing in evolving the shape of the new fighter. In the early 1930s the wind tunnels we had available were all rather small and there tended to be a lot of turbulence, which meant that the results were not all that reliable. In the case of the Type 224, for example, the flight trials revealed that the fighter had a performance somewhat different from that which the wind tunnel tests had led us to expect. In the case of the F.37/34 we went through each of the drag-producing features of the Type 224, and tried to eliminate them one by one. In effect we said: we know this is better; we know we have transferred a fault on the Type 224 to a non-fault on the new design; so there is little point in going back to first principles and testing each new feature in the wind tunnel. In fact the only part of the F.37/34 which was tested in the wind tunnel during the design stage of the aircraft was the underwing radiator duct.

Specification F.37/34 had called for a four-gun fighter, like its predecessor. But when the wooden mock-up was finished the Air Ministry changed its mind and asked if we could fit in eight guns. After a bit of a struggle we managed to squeeze all eight into our thin wing, with just a hint of a bulge round the two outer weapons.

Throughout the design work on the new fighter, none of us gave much thought to the idea of mass-production. In 1935 a major war was a long way from most peoples' minds and the most the company could hope for was an order from the Royal Air Force for twenty-five or perhaps fifty, plus a few sold abroad. Had we had mass-production in mind for the Spitfire from the beginning, we should almost certainly have arranged the internal structure rather differently; but in my view the external shape of the aeroplane would have been pretty much the same.

Once the design work on the new fighter was complete, we on the design team were virtually finished with it and we moved on to Mitchell's next project: a four-engined bomber to Air Ministry Specification B.12/36. Then, in 1938, I left Supermarine to take up a post at the Air Ministry. My part in the Spitfire story was over.

Looking back over my time with the Supermarine design team, I remember it as one of the happiest of my life. We were all young men, tackling the problems with the enthusiasm that goes with youth. Over us stood Reginald Mitchell, a stimulating taskmaster. Now, more than forty years later, it is nice to think that a few people have a slight interest in what we did.

Appendix A.

SPECIFICATION No F. 7/30

1st October 1931

Single Seater Day and Night Fighter

1. General Requirements

(a) The aircraft is to fulfill the duties of "Single Seater Fighter" for day and night flying. A satisfactory fighting view is essential and designers should consider the advantages offered in this respect by low wing monoplane or pusher.

The main requirements for the aircraft are:
 (i) Highest possible rate of climb
 (ii) Highest possible speed at 15,000 feet
 (iii) Fighting view
 (iv) Manoeuvrability
 (v) Capability of easy and rapid production in quantity
 (vi) Ease of maintenance.

(b) The aircraft must have a good degree of positive stability about all axes in flight and trimming gear must be fitted so that the tail incidence can be adjusted in flight to ensure that the aircraft will fly horizontally at all speeds within the flying range, without requiring attention from the pilot.

(c) When carrying the total load specified in paragraph 3, the aircraft must be fully controllable at all flying speeds, especially near the stall and during a steep dive, when there must be no tendency for the aircraft to hunt.

(d) The aircraft must have a high degree of manoeuvrability. It must answer all controls quickly and must not be tiring to fly. The control must be adequate to stop an incipient spin when the aircraft is stalled.

An approved type of slot control, or other means which will ensure adequate lateral control and stability, at and below stalling speed, is to be embodied.

The design of the aileron control is to be such that operation of the ailerons in flight will produce the minimum of adverse yawing effect on the aircraft.

(e) The aircraft is to be designed to accomodate the equipment listed in paragraph 6 and scheduled in detail in the Appendix "A" [not included] to this Specification.

(f) The crew, armament and equipment are to be arranged as specified in paragraph 7 of this Specification.

(g) The arrangements for alighting and taking off must be as specified in paragraph 8 of this Specification.

(h) The aircraft and all parts thereof are to be designed and constructed in conformity with the requirements of the Director of Technical Development, Air Ministry.

A "Type Record" for the aircraft, including all drawings and a complete set of strength calculations and weight estimates must be submitted to the Director of Technical Development or his authorised representative for acceptance. The contractor, pending acceptance, may proceed with construction if he so desires, but the Director of Technical Development reserves the right to reject any part or parts so made if subsequently found to be under strength or otherwise unsuitable for H. M. Service.

Two copies of fully-dimensioned General Arrangement drawing to the aircraft as actually built, together with a General Arrangement drawing showing the layout of the complete equipment, are to be supplied to the Director of Technical Development (R.D.A3) immediately on the completion of the first aircraft. Similarly in the case of any subsequent aircraft if differing from the first.

(i) The aircraft is to be constructed throughout in metal and is to be constructed and protected as to adequately withstand sudden changes in temperature and humidity such as are experienced in semi-tropical climates. Streamline wires, tie-rods and other parts not of stainless steel are to be coated with cadmium or zinc by an approved process. Aluminium and aluminium alloy parts are to be anodically treated.

(j) As soon as possible after the mock-up conference the contractor is to supply to the Director of Technical Development (R.D.4.) a General Arrangement Drawing of the engine installation (including fuel, oil and water systems, tankage and engine controls). (See also paragraph 10).

(k) On the completion of the first aircraft off the contract the contractor shall supply to the Director of Technical Development such details of the equipment and its accessories and the detail weights, length and quantities thereof as will enable the Appendix "A" Schedule of Equipment to be completed.

This information is to be supplied by amending a copy of the current Appendix "A" to agree with the approved aircraft, in conformity with the current master schedule.

Similarly, on the delivery of the last aircraft off the contract, if alterations have been made to the equipment, a suitably amended copy of the current Appendix "A" is to be supplied to the Director of Technical Development.

(l) All materials used must, where possible, be to B.E.S.A. or other standard Specifications as approved by the Director of Technical Development.

All materials quoted under approved Specifications are to be to the latest issue of the Specification. A list of approved Specifications showing the latest issue numbers may be obtained on application in writing to the Director of Technical Development.

Similarly, all A.G.S. parts incorporated in the aircraft are to be to the latest approved issue of the appropriate drawings but the issue number should not be quoted on the aircraft drawing. Where the contractor proposes to use materials for which standard approved Specifications are not available, the contractor is required to notify the Director of Technical Development, in writing, of his intention, and to supply such information and test pieces of the materials proposed as the Director of Technical Development may deem necessary, to enable adequate tests of the materials to be carried out.

(m) Two copies of rigging and maintenance notes are to be supplied to the Director of Technical Development (R.T.P.) not later than the date on which the first aircraft is delivered to the experimental establishment.

In order to facilitate further reproduction of any diagrams contained in the notes, tracings thereof are to be supplied also.

The note should anticipate any difficulty likely to be encountered by the Service Unit during the development of a new type and are to include:-

(i) leading particulars, principal dimensions, and the capacities of fuel and oil tanks in tabular form;
(ii) complete and detailed instructions for rigging the aircraft;
(iii) any unusual features (including non-standard equipment) from the point of view of maintenance;
(iv) lubrication instructions;
(v) description of the engine mounting and installation in so far as they are peculiar to the particular aircraft;
(vi) three-view general arrangement drawings (showing the horizontal datum line on the side view) and diagrams of the petrol and oil systems;
(vii) the approved equipment layout drawings as called for in paragraph 10 (d).

It is to be observed that these notes are required only for a preliminary guide for those who will be responsible for maintaining the aircraft in its early stages and it will suffice if they are written on the lines of a works instruction.

In the event of the aircraft being adopted for use in the Royal Air Force the contractor will be required to prepare notes and drawings covering the repair of the aircraft by Service Units.

2. Power Unit

(a) Any approved British engine may be used. It is to be noted that, when an engine is in process of development, provision is to be made in the aircraft design for a possible increase in engine weight.

(b) The installation of the engine is to be so arranged that the engine is capable of being rapidly and easily removed from the aircraft.

Supports and footholds are to be provided to facilitate minor repairs and adjustments to be the engine installation.

(c) The whole of the cowling is to be designed to facilitate rapid and easy removal and replacement and is to be sufficiently robust to withstand frequent removal and constant handling; wire skewers are not to be used.

(d) The cowling is to be finished in an approved manner so as to give adequate protection against corrosion and to prevent the reflection of light which might betray the presence of the aircraft or dazzle the crew.

(e) Before drawings relative to the engine installation can be accepted the engine, fuel, oil and water systems, and the accessories and piping therefore, must be fitted in the first experimental aircraft and put in proper running order, so that the installation as a whole may be examined and, if satisfactory, approved by the Director of Technical Development, or his authorised representative.

(f) The airscrew is preferably to be of metal construction, and is to be designed in accordance with the required performance of the aircraft as specified in paragraph 4 of this Specification, but no airscrew will be accepted which allows the maximum permissible r.p.m. to be exceeded in full throttle horizontal flight at the supercharged altitude of the engine, or the normal r.p.m. to be exceeded in full throttle climbing flight at the best rate of climb above this altitude.

A standard engine instruction plate is to be fitted in a position where it will be clearly visible to the pilot.

2. (A) Tankage including gravity tanks to be provided for the endurance specified in paragraph 3.

(a) Adequate air space is to be provided in the oil tank: at least 1 gallon for air-cooled engines and 2 gallons for water-cooled engines.

(b) A gravity fuel tank is to be provided sufficient for at least 20 minutes at full throttle at ground level.

(c) The fuel tanks are to be adequately protected from deterioration in a manner approved by the Director of Technical Development and may be either:-

(i) Carried inside the fuselage
or
(ii) Carried inside the main planes. In this case the construction of the portions of the main planes containing the fuel tanks and the installation of the fuel tanks therein must be such that there can be no possibility of escaping fuel or fuel vapour from a damaged tank spreading to any inflammable portions of the aircraft structure
or
(iii) Carried externally in such a position that if damaged the escaping fuel will be blown clear of all parts of the aircraft structure when in flight.

(d) All tanks are to be provided with readily removable sumps or with approved means of removing all dirt and foreign matter from the interior of the tank.

(e) The delivery from the tank to the piping system is to be so arranged as to prevent as far as is practicable the passage of foreign matter from the tank into the piping system.

Means are to be provided, under the control of a member of the crew, for stopping and restarting the flow from any of the fuel tanks at each outlet from which the fuel would otherwise escape if the pipe line or balance pipe connected therewith were to break.

(f) Arrangements are to be made for the rapid and easy draining of the tanks, and rapid and easy filling with standard filler nozzles.

(g) All tanks are to be designed to be readily removable from and replaceable in position in the aircraft, with a minimum of disturbance to the aircraft structure and to other installations.

2. (B) Fuel and Oil Systems

(a) The fuel and oil systems shall be in general accordance with the requirements of Specification No 18 (Misc)

(b) All pipe joints are to be of approved metallic type, and together will all cocks, plugs, etc., are to be locked in accordance with A.G.S. Mod 157.

(c) The bore of the main fuel pipes must be such that the flow of fuel sufficient to maintain full power on the ground is exceeded by 100 per cent when the carburetter unions are uncoupled and the supply is in the condition of minimum head with the aircraft set at the appropriate angle so defined hereunder in clause (d) (i).

The last section of the delivery pipe to the carburetters is to be of the approved flexible type.

(d) The fuel feed may be either :-
  (i) By approved fuel pumps from the main tanks direct to the carburetters with a by-pass to a gravity tank, so situated that, when the aircraft is flying at its maximum climbing angle, or when the aircraft is tail down on the ground, whichever condition gives the greatest inclination of the aircraft axis to the horizontal, the minimum effective head above the jet level of the highest carburetter when the gravity tank is practically empty is not less than the minimum specified for the type of carburetter used.

In calculating the minimum effective head due allowance must be made for any effect due to acceleration when the aircraft is in motion.

The delivery from the pumps to the carburetter must be via an approved release or reducing valve to a distributer cock or cocks so arranged that the following selections can be made.
  (1) Pumps to carburetters and gravity tanks
  (2) Pumps to carburetters direct
  (3) Gravity tanks to carburetters
  (4) Off
Wind driven pumps are not to be used.

An overflow pipe of sufficient bore to deal with all excess fuel must be provided from the gravity tank to the main tank or to some other approved point in the fuel system.

A prismatic flow indicator visible to the pilot is to be fitted in the overflow pipe
                          or
  (ii) By gravity tanks alone feeding direct to the carburetter. Such gravity tanks must conform to the requirements laid down in (i) above.

(e) A diagram of the fuel system is to be affixed in an approved position in the aircraft.

(f) An approved type of petrol filter is to be fitted so that the whole of the fuel passes through it before reaching the carburetter. The filter must be disposed so that it will be accessible for cleaning.

2. (C) Cooling Systems

(a) Provision is to be made for adequate oil cooling and a thermometer registering in a position visible to the pilot is to be fitted in such a position as to indicate the temperature of the oil supplied to the engine.

In addition, on the first aircraft, an oil thermometer registering in a position visible to the pilot, is to be fitted in the return pipe from the engine between the scavenger pump and the oil cooler.

(b) If a water or evaporating engine is used, the cooling system, which is to be installed in accordance with the requirements of D.T.D., is to be designed to fulfil English summer requirements, with provision for changing to a system fulfilling Tropical summer requirements, with a minimum of alteration. If water indicators are used they are to be fitted with shutters or other approved means of temperature control.

(c) In addition to the thermometer fittings and thermometers normally required on radiators for production aircraft, the experimental aircraft is to be provided with approved thermometer fittings in the outlet header tanks or each radiator or auxiliary radiator.

2. (D) Engine Starting and Silencing

(a) The exhaust manifold of approved type supplied with the engine is to be fitted in such a manner as to provide adequately for silencing, and for flame-damping during night flying.

(b) Provision is to be made on the aircraft by the installation of the requisite approved fittings for the installation of an R.A.E. Mark II Starter and for the rapid and easy attachment of a compressor type engine starter carried on a separate trolley.

(c) Provision is to be made for rapidly warming the engine oil. It must be possible to take off within $2\frac{1}{2}$ minutes from a cold start.

3. Load to be carried

In addition to any stowages and mountings necessitated by the requirements of paragraphs 6 and 7 and by alternative loads, the following load is to be carried during the acceptance flights :-

	Removable	Fixed	Total
Crew (1)	180	—	180 lb
Oxygen	15	8	23
Instruments	1	25	26
R/T Apparatus	46	6	52
Electrical Equipment	41	17	58
Parachute and belt	20	3	23
Armament			
4 guns and C.C. gear*	120	20	140
Gun sights	—	5	5
200 rounds S.A.A.	145	—	145
Signal Pistol & Cartridges	7	1	8
Military Load;	575	85	660 lb

*This item will be adjusted to the actual gun installation adopted

Fuel	For $\frac{1}{2}$ hour at full throttle at
Oil	ground level, plus 2.0 hours at full
Water (if required).	throttle at 15,000'.
	Oil—ditto plus 50% excess.
	Water—ditto.

4. Contract Performance

The performance of the aircraft, as ascertained during the official type trials when carrying the total load specified in paragraph 3 and with an airscrew satisfying the requirements of paragraph 2 (e) shall be :-

Horizontal speed at 15,000 ft not less than 195 mph
alighting speed not to exceed   60 mph
Service ceiling not less than   28,000 ft
Time to 15,000 ft not more than $8\frac{1}{2}$ mins

The specified alighting speed must not be exceeded, but may be obtained by variable camber or equivalent devices provided that control and manoeuvrability are not adversely affected.

5. Structural Strength

(a) The strength of the main structure when carrying the load specified in paragraph 3, plus 100 lb shall not be less than as defined hereunder:-

Load factor throughout the structure with the centre of pressure in the most forward position: 9.0

Load factor for wing structure with the centre of pressure in its most backward position in horizontal flight 6.0

Load factor in a terminal nose dive: 1.75

Inverted Flight

(1) Load factor at incidence corresponding to the inverted stall and with C.P. at 1/3 of the chord: 4.5

(2) Load factor at incidence appropriate to steady horizontal inverted flight and at the maximum speed of horizontal normal flight: 4.5

(b) The alighting gear must be able to withstand an impact at a vertical velocity of 10 feet per second and at this velocity the load on the alighting gear must not exceed three times the fully loaded weight of the aircraft.

(c) When subject to the impact forces on alighting, as specified above, the load factor for the alighting gear must not be less than 1–1/3, and for the remainder of the structure not less than 1–1/2. The load factor for the structure and the attachment fittings of the alighting gear must always be greater than that for the alighting gear itself by the margin indicated above.

(d) The maximum weight per wheel of the aircraft in pounds must not exceed 12 times the product of the wheel and tyre diameters in inches with the aircraft carrying the full load specified above.

(e) The above factors are to be determined by the approved official methods as published by the Directorate of Technical Development and the detail requirements given in A.P. 970 are also to be satisfied. With a view to minimising the risk of flutter, attention should be given to the recommendations of R. & M. 1177, particularly as regards the static balance of ailerons.

(f) The wing is to be sufficiently rigid to withstand satisfactorily any torsional or other loads which may be encountered during service operations.

(g) Ribs (both main plane and tail unit) are required to develop, on test, factors 20 per cent greater than those specified for the aircraft as a whole.

6. Equipment

The equipment as listed hereunder and as scheduled in detail in the Appendix "A" to this Specification is to be provided for and the contractor will be required to supply and fit all parts necessary for its installation; in the case of R/T panels, etc., etc., the position for all instruments and the identities of plugs and leads must be indicated by fixed labels.

It is to be noted that the weights of various items of fixed equipment listed hereunder and scheduled in detail in the Appendix "A", but not quoted in paragraph 3, are to be allowed for in design.

Diagrams of the wiring and piping for all equipment installations are to be provided, for carrying in a canvas bag fitted in an approved position on the aircraft.

All equipment is to be installed in accordance with the requirements of the Director of Technical Development.

(a) Armament

Reflector sight	(To be installed
Ring and Bead Sight	in accordance with
Signal Pistol and 8 cartridges	Specification
4 × 20 lb bombs	No G.E. 126

2 × .303" Vickers guns installed in the cockpit under the control of the pilot with C.C. gear as necessary.

and either:-

(i) 2 × .303" Vickers guns installed in the cockpit or wings. If in the cockpit and synchronised an additional C.C. gear reservoir is to be fitted for them. If in the wings adequate locating arrangements are essential.

or:-

(ii) 2 × .303" Lewis guns installed so that synchronisation is unnecessary. These guns do not require heating. 2000 rounds of ammunition for the above guns with links or drums as necessary. The minimum supply to be forwarded for any gun is 400 rounds. 400 round drums will be available for Lewis guns.

(b) Electrical Equipment

Services are to be provided for:	(To be installed in
Navigation and Identification Lights	accordance with
Gun Heaters	Specification
(as necessary for outboard guns)	No G.E. 164)
Wing tip flares	
(on concealed brackets)	
Instrument Lighting	

(c) Instruments and General Equipment

The following instruments (of luminous pattern, where available) are to be fitted in the cockpit in accordance with the requirements of the Director of Technical Development:-

1 Air Speed Indicator
1 Altimeter
1 Revolution Indicator
1 Oil Pressure Gauge
Fuel Contents Gauge (1 per main tank)
1 Oil Thermometer (An extra oil thermometer is required on the first aircraft).
1 Radiator Thermometer (if required). An extra water thermometer is required on the first aircraft.
Boost Gauge (if required)
1 Watch and Holder
1 Compass
1 Pilot's Fighting Harness (Sutton Type)
Oxygen Apparatus
1 Map Case
1 Turn Indicator

(d) Wireless Equipment

Earth System, Bonding and Screening in accordance with Specification G.E. 125.
R/T Apparatus (Two-way)
R/T Box
Fixed Aerial.

(e) Parachute Equipment
1 Irving type Parachute

7. Disposition of Crew, Armament and Equipment

(a) The Pilot's view is to conform as closely as possible to that obtainable in "pusher" aircraft. The following requirements indicate the ideal view which is considered to be necessary, and the aircraft should be designed to conform as closely to them as is possible in practice.

(b) The pilot must have a clear view forward and upward for formation work and manoeuvring, and particular care is needed to prevent his view of hostile aircraft being blanked out by top planes and centre sections when manoeuvring to attack. Planes should be so disposed as not to obstruct the pilot's view of other aircraft, when his own is pointing within 60° of their direction.

The direction in which obstruction by planes is least serious is in the backward and downward directions.

(c) For landing a good view forward and downward is necessary, and the pilot must be able to see within 17° from the vertical over the side when wearing the Sutton harness.

The point on the ground on which the pilot desires to land should not be obstructed by planes during the gliding approach. This applies especially to normal landing manoeuvres such as banked turns and side slips.

The windscreen should be sufficiently high to enable the pilot to have a clear view forward through the screen. When taxying with the tail down the pilot, with minimum movement of his head, should be able to see directly in front of his aircraft, while with tail up for taking off he should be able to see the ground 50 feet ahead over the centre line of the aircraft, with his seat in the normal flying position. The top fuselage coaming, on either side of the windscreen, should be as narrow and tapered as possible consistent with adequate protection from the slipstream.

(d) For gun aiming purposes the pilot should have an unobstructed view forward over as wide a cone as possible the sight being the axis of that cone with his eye the apex.

(e) The pilot is to be provided with 4 guns, and stowage for 2000 rounds of ammunition as detailed in paragraph 6(a).

Provision is to be made for fitting of a G.3 camera gun complete with firing and cocking controls. The mounting and controls must be quickly removable and must not interfere with the guns and sights in any way. This provision is secondary and must not influence the design of the aircraft in any way.

(f) The pilot is to be provided with a map case, and stowage for knee-type writing pad mounted in a convenient position.

(g) The relative positions of the pilot's seat and rudder bar are to be designed to be adjustable both vertically and horizontally to suit pilots of different trunk length and leg reach.

(h) The design of the cockpit must be such as to provide the comfort necessary for the pilot to fulfil his various duties efficiently, and must allow complete freedom of movement, particularly in an emergency that obliges the pilot to take to his parachute.

The cockpit is to be adequately screened from the wind but the windscreen must not interfere with the satisfactory use of sights, one of which should be on the centre line of the aircraft, the sights being interchangeable in position.

The cockpit is to be painted internally with an approved grey-green paint. This instruction does not apply to the instrument board.

The cockpit padding and other upholstery is to be rendered fireproof to the satisfaction of the Director of Technical Development.

(i) Standard clips are to be provided under the wings for the carrying of one standard bomb rack for 4 × 20 lb bombs.

Room is to be provided to enable the bomb release gear for these bombs to be fitted inside on the port side of the cockpit.

The arrangement of the bomb carrier installation must be such that sufficient clearance is provided to enable the bombs to be released even when the aircraft is in a very steep dive.

(j) Arrangements are to be made to provide adequate cockpit heating without resort to electrical applicances.

(k) The dynamo for the electrical equipment is to be stowed internally and driven from the engine. The aircraft designer must agree the details of the drive with the engine designer.

8. Arrangements for alighting and taking off

(a) The aircraft is to be designed to pull up quickly on alighting and wheel brakes of an approved type are to be fitted.

The brake controls shall be such that the brakes can be applied together or independently. It is essential that the pilot shall not be obliged to abandon the aircraft or engine controls when applying the brakes. Means are to be provided for locking the brakes in the "on" position so that wheel chocks may be dispensed with if so desired. The whole of the braking system is to be capable of rapid and easy removal when not required.

(b) The aircraft is to be suitable for operation from small, rough-surfaced and enclosed aerodromes.

(c) The alighting gear is to be of oleo or equivalent type in which the use of rubber in tension is eliminated.

(d) The wheel track of the alighting gear must be such as to provide stable taxying conditions in any direction in a wind of 20 mph without any tendency for the aircraft to capsize.

(e) The wheels of the alighting gear are to be provided with approved means for lubricating the wheel bearings, which are to be designed so that no wear takes place on the axle.

(f) The design and disposition of the alighting gear are to be such as to allow of the aircraft being readily and securely supported without the use of elaborate jacking, trestling or slinging during and subsequent to the removal of the alighting gear or the wheels of the alighting gear. If necessary, special arrangements are to be made in the design of the aircraft structure to permit of such support being readily given and the points of support so specially provided must be clearly marked on the aircraft.

9. Miscellaneous

(a) The aircraft is to be constructed in quickly detachable units for ease of transport and storage.

(b) Means are to be provided for locking the slats in the closed position and maintaining the controls in a central position when the aircraft is left unattended on the ground. The means so provided must preclude the possibility of the pilot attempting to take-off with the slats and/or the controls locked.

(c) Suitable holding-down rings are to be provided under the bottom planes.

(d) The aircraft is to be provided with all necessary handgrips and other facilities for ease of handling on the ground.

(e) Provision is to be made in the design for the protection of all moving parts against the destructive effects of sand and, as far as may be possible, for their lubrication by grease gun from a central point.

(f) Detachable covers of approved type are to be supplied for the engine and cockpit as a protection against deterioration when the aircraft is pegged down in the open.

(g) The attachment points for the pilot's fighting harness together with those parts of the aircraft to which the belt loads are transmitted are to be capable of withstanding the failing load of the belt or harness.

(h) The design of the structure in the vicinity of the cockpit is to be such as to afford the pilot as much protection as possible in the event of a heavy landing, or crash or overturning.

Such structure should be appreciably stronger than the adjacent parts so that these latter may absorb some of the shock by deformation before the former yields.

(i) The design of the aircraft is to be such that standard Service equipment can be used for ground operations such as fuelling, rigging, manhandling, etc. Particulars of service ground equipment can be obtained on application in writing to the Director of Technical Development (R.D.A.5.).

(j) The design and layout of the aircraft is to be such as to offer every facility for rapid and easy inspection and maintenance in service and, in general, is to permit of maintenance operations being performed with standard Service equipment. Special equipment (including tools) shall be provided with the aircraft if an essential supply, but the introduction of non-standard articles is to be avoided whenever possible.

(k) Parts that require to be frequently replaced or inspected are to be easily accessible, and fully visible to a mechanic working on them.

(l) Control cables are to be arranged so that the deterioration due to wear is a minimum. Means are to be provided to facilitate the fitting of new cable and its rapid threading through fairleads. The splicing of cable in place is prohibited.

(m) Positive-locking devices shall be provided for all joints and fastenings; such devices are to be rapidly and easily adjustable.

(n) Adequate facilities are to be provided for inspecting the fuselage interior and working parts, particularly those of the tail skid and tail plane adjusting gear.

(o) Arrangements are to be made for defining the position of the centre of gravity in accordance with Aircraft Design Memorandum No 205.

10. Provision of Mock-up

(a) In order that the proposed disposition of the crew, armament etc., may be properly examined and approved by the Director of Technical Development before construction is commenced the contractor is required to provide suitable "mock-up" of the aircraft at his works. The "mock-up" so provided must include all parts and components which are likely to interfere with the all-round view from the cockpit and must shew the internal arrangements of the cockpit and such details of the engine installation as the arrangements for engine-starting and the positions of cocks, pumps, etc.

(b) The "mock-up" must be erected full size and must be constructed true to scale and all instruments and equipment must be represented full size.

(c) The "mock-up" must be capable of being inclined at angles corresponding to the cruising and alighting attitudes of the aircraft and to this end must be constructed to the correct height from the ground.

(d) Within 10 days of the mock-up conference the contractor is to submit to the Director of Technical Development (R.D.A.4.) two copies of provisional drawings of the layout as decided at the mock-up.

Four copies of the layout drawings as finally approved are to be supplied to the Director of Technical Development (R.D.A.) 4).

These equipment layout drawings are to be a 1/8th scale and are to consist of skeleton views of the fuselage and other pertinent structure shewing views of all equipment:

(1) positioned on the starboard side of the aircraft, viewed from the inside;
(2) positioned on the port side, viewed from inside;
(3) positioned in plan, together with
(4) full views of instrument boards, W/T panels, etc. and
(5) a schedule of equipment indexed to correspond to "balloon" pointers (a spare column is to be provided for notes or alterations).

Each of the drawings is to shew also seats, tanks, controls, etc. appropriate to each view.

In accordance with the procedure laid down in Aircraft Design Memorandum No 135 the contractor is to supply a bare W/T panel as and when required.

11. Test Specimens

(a) The Contractor will be required to supply and ordinarily test (see clause (d)) such specimens of parts of the aircraft as the Director of Technical Development may consider should be tested in order to ensure that the design and construction of the aircraft will be satisfactory.

(b) Tenders for the supply of aircraft in accordance with this specification are to include a Schedule of the specimens and tests considered sufficient to meet the requirements of clause (a) and are to cover the cost of supplying and testing the specimens. Any schedule that is considered by the Director of Technical Development to be inadequate will be returned to the firm concerned for amendment.

(c) The specimens and tests that will generally be essential are indicated hereunder:

Complete ribs.	The specimens are to be tested under the conditions of normal flight and, when appropriate, inverted flight. Metal ribs will be required to undergo, in addition, a vibration test.
Metal spars.	The specimens will be submitted to the standard test, if applicable, and otherwise to such test as the Director of Technical Development may require.

(d) Except as provided for hereafter, the testing shall be done by the Contractor, or he shall arrange for it to be done at some approved Testing Establishment; in either case, due notice of the time and place of the tests shall be given to the Director of Technical Development so that he may arrange for a representative to witness them; the conditions governing the tests are to be in accordance with the requirements of the Director of Technical Development and the tests are to be performed to his satisfaction; reports on the tests are to be supplied to the Director of Technical Development in duplicate. If neither of the aforementioned arrangements is possible, the tests will be done at the Royal Aircraft Establishment, at the Contractor's expense.

(e) The Director of Technical Development reserves the right to call for specimens and tests additional to those referred to in the Contractor's Schedule, should he at any time after the placing of the contract consider them to be necessary.

(f) No specimen of any part of the aircraft shall be submitted for testing without it being previously certified by the Inspector-in-Charge at the Contractor's works, that the specimen is typical, as regards materials, dimensions, limits and workmanship of the actual part.

(g) A thin coat of oil or vaseline may be applied to metal specimens to prevent corrosion. Varnish, enamel or similar substances must not be used for this purpose.

12. Provision of Drawings for a Model

If at any time the Director of Technical Development shall so desire, the contractor shall supply the drawings and data necessary for the construction of a true-to-scale model of the complete aircraft suitable for aerodynamic trials in a wind tunnel; such drawings, if required, would form the subject of an amendment to contract.

13. Publication of Test Results

The Director of Technical Development reserves the right to

publish data contained in reports of any wind tunnel or other tests relating to the design of the aircraft which may be undertaken on his behalf.

14. Pre-acceptance Test Flights

(a) Prior to the delivery of the aircraft to the Departmental Establishment at which the Type Trials are to take place it shall have been certified to the Director of Technical Development:

    (i) That the aircraft has been subjected by the contractor's pilot to the flight tests referred to in the "Statement of Special Contract Conditions" accompanying the contract and

    (ii) that these tests have shewn that the aircraft is safe to be flown by pilots of the Royal Air Force.

(b) The tests referred to in (a) shall include:-

    (i) A demonstration that the aircraft may be spun, both to the right and to the left, without undue risk when loaded in accordance with paragraph (3) of the Specification, and with the Centre of Gravity at the aft authorised limit. For this purpose it is required that the aircraft, after being put into a spin, shall be allowed to complete not less than eight turns before the pilot sets his controls for recovery. The aircraft will be deemed satisfactory as regards its behaviour in a spin if the height loss in recovery does not exceed 1500 feet. This height loss is to be reckoned from when the pilot sets his controls for recovery until the aircraft "flattens out" from the landing dive.

    (ii) A dive to the terminal velocity.

    (iii) A demonstration of satisfactory behaviour during normal aerobatics such as the loop, roll, stalled turns, etc.

AIR MINISTRY
Directorate of Technical Development

Appendix B.

SUPERMARINE SPECIFICATION No 425a
26th July 1934

**Supermarine Day and Night Fighter to Air Ministry
Specification F.7/30
Proposed Modifications**

Arrangement

It is proposed to modify the existing aeroplane by building a new pair of wings incorporating a retracting chassis. The new wings are of reduced area, the present inner sections of negative dihedral being dispensed with. Split trailing-edge flaps are provided to increase the lift and thus retain the same landing speed. The existing aircraft is shown on Drawing No 22400, Sheet 1 and the proposed arrangement on Drawing No 30000, Sheet 2.

Construction

Construction is greatly simplified by making each wing in one piece. Other features which simplify construction are the substitution of lattice for a plate web, enabling the riveting of the nose to be more easily carried out, and the provision of smooth in place of corrugated covering.

Pilot's View

As a result of eliminating the downward-sloping wing roots, the view for a pilot is not quite so good close in to the fuselage, but is improved further out by the reduction of span.

Main Particulars and Dimensions

	Existing Machine	Modified Machine
Span	45 ft 10 ins	39 ft 4 ins
Length Overall	29 ft 10 ins	29 ft 4 ins
Wing Area (gross)	295 sq ft	255 sq ft
Wing Loading	16.8 lb sq ft	18.4 lb sq ft
Power Loading	8.25 lb/bhp	7.85 lb/bhp

Weight and Performance

It is estimated that the proposed modifications will result in a saving of 250 pounds weight, and an improvement in top speed of 30 mph, the climb remaining practically unaltered. The following features giving the comparisons between the existing and the modified aeroplanes, are estimated. Performance tests so far carried out are incomplete, but present indications are that the estimates are reasonably correct.

	Existing Machine	Modified Machine
Weight	4,950 pounds	4,700 pounds
Max. Speed	235 mph	265 mph
Climb to 15,000 ft	8 mins	$8\frac{1}{4}$ mins

SPECIFICATION F.37/34
3rd January 1935

Experimental High Speed Single Seat Fighter
(Supermarine Aviation Works)

---

1. General

This specification is intended to cover the design and construction of an experimental high speed single seat fighter substantially as described in the Supermarine Specification No 425a and drawing No 30000 Sheet 13, except that an improvement in the pilot's view is desirable. The aircraft shall conform to all the requirements stated in Specification F.7/30 and all corregenda thereto, except as stated hereunder.

2. Power Unit

(a) The engine to be installed shall be the Rolls Royce P.V.XII

(b) The airscrew shall be of wooden construction. The Provisions of Para 2(f) of Specification F.7/30 as regards the provision for the effect of a metal airscrew on weight and C. of G. movement can be ignored.

(c) The fuel system shall be in accordance with DTD Specification No DTD 1004. A duplicate engine-driven system may be used.

(d) A cooling system is to be of the evaporative cooling type, using wing condensers in association with an auxiliary radiator.

(e) Hand starting gear only is provided for engine starting.

3. Load to be Carried

The service load shall be as defined in Specification F.7/30, except for departures which may subsequently be agreed between the contractor and the Director of Technical Development. The fuel load to be carried is to be 94 gallons

with oil appropriate to the endurance implied by this fuel.

4. Equipment and Miscellaneous

(a) Non-standard navigation lights of the type approved by DTD may be fitted, and will be supplied by the contractor.

(b) The requirement for Para 8(a) of Specification F.7/30 that the braking system is to be capable of rapid and easy removal is to be deleted.

(c) The reference to the hand holds or other aids to the handling at the wing tips of Para 9(d) of Specification F.7/30 is to be altered to read: "Internal provision is to be made for taking holding-down guys at the wing tips. Hand holds or grips will not be necessary."

(d) The requirement for Para 6 as regards gun installation is modified. All four guns may be installed outside the airscrew disc.

(e) Tail wheel is to be fitted if practicable.

5. Structural Strength

(a) Para 5(d) of Specification F.7/30 is to be altered to read: "The alighting gear must be able to withstand an impact at a vertical velocity of 10 feet per second, and at this velocity the load on the alighting gear must not exceed $4\frac{1}{2}$ times the fully-loaded weight of the aircraft."

(b) Wheels not conforming with Para 5(d) of Specification F.7/30 will be accepted, but the actual size and type proposed must be approved by the Director of Technical Development.

44

Appendix D.

REQUIREMENTS FOR
SINGLE-ENGINE SINGLE-SEATER DAY AND
NIGHT FIGHTER (F.10/35)
April 1935

1. General
The Air Staff require a single-engine single-seater day and night fighter which can fulfil the following conditions:-
  (a) Have a speed in excess of the contemporary bomber of at least 40 mph at 15,000 ft.
  (b) Have a number of forward firing machine guns that can produce the maximum hitting power possible in the short space of time available for one attack. To attain this object it is proposed to mount as many guns as possible and it is considered that eight guns should be provided. The requirements are given in more detail below.

2. Performance
  (a) Speed. The maximum possible and not less than 310 mph at 15,000 ft at maximum power with the highest speed possible between 5,000 and 15,000 ft.
  (b) Climb. The best possible to 20,000 ft but secondary to speed and hitting power.
  (c) Service Ceiling. Not less than 30,000 ft is desirable.
  (d) Endurance. $\frac{1}{4}$ hour at maximum power at sea level plus 1 hour at maximum power at which engine can be run continuously at 15,000 ft. This should provide $\frac{1}{2}$ hour at maximum power at which engine can be run continously (for climb etc.), plus 1 hour at most economic speed at 15,000 ft (for patrol), plus $\frac{1}{4}$ hour at maximum power at 15,000 ft (for attack). To allow for possible increase in engine power during the life of this aircraft, tankage is to be provided to cover $\frac{1}{4}$ hour at maximum power at sea level plus $1\frac{1}{4}$ hours at maximum power at which engine can run continuously at 15,000 ft.
  (e) Take off and landing. The aircraft to be capable of taking off and landing over a 50 ft barrier in a distance of 500 yards.

3. Armament
Not less than 6 guns, but 8 guns are desirable. These should be located outside the airscrew disc. Re-loading in the air is not required and the guns should be fired by electrical or means other than Bowden wire.
  It is contemplated that some or all of these guns should be mounted to permit of a degree of elevation and traverse with some form of control from the pilot's seat. Though it is not at present possible to give details, it is desirable that designers should be aware of the possibility of this development, which should not, however, be allowed to delay matters at this stage.

4. Ammunition
300 rounds per gun if eight guns are provided and 400 rounds per gun if only six guns are installed.

5. View
  (a) The upper hemisphere must be, so far as possible, unobstructed to the view of the pilot to facilitate search and attack. A good view for formation flying is required, both for formation leader and flank aircraft and for night landing.
  (b) A field of view of about 10° downwards from the horizontal line of sight over the nose is required for locating the target.

6. Handling
  (a) A high degree of manoeuvrability at high speeds is not required but good control at low speeds is essential.
  (b) A minimum alteration of tail trim with variations of throttle settings is required.
  (c) The aircraft must be a steady firing platform.

7. Special Features and Equipment
  (a) Enclosed cockpit
  (b) Cockpit heating
  (c) Night flying equipment.
  (d) R/T.
  (e) Oxygen for $2\frac{1}{2}$ hours.
  (f) Guns to be easily accessible on the ground for loading and maintenance.
  (g) Retractable undercarriage and tailwheel permissible.
  (h) Wheel brakes.
  (j) Engine starting. If an electric starter is provided a ground accumulator will be used with a plug-in point on the aircraft—an accumulator for this purpose is not required to be carried in the aircraft. The actual starting must be under control of the pilot. In addition hand turning gear is required.

Appendix E.

**AEROPLANE AND ARMAMENT
EXPERIMENTAL ESTABLISHMENT
MARTLESHAM HEATH**
September 1936

Handling trials of the
Spitfire K-5054

A.M. Ref:- 431708/35/R.D.A.1.
A.&A.E.E. Ref:- M/4493/20—A.S. 56

Handling trials were done at a total weight of 5332 lb, the centre of gravity was 9.7 inches aft of the datum point.

Limits 8.25″–9.9″ aft—extended by .01 chord to 10.8 inches aft.

CONTROLS

Ailerons
On the ground the aileron control works freely and without play. Full movement of the control column can be obtained when the pilot is in the cockpit.

In the air the ailerons are light to handle when climbing and on the glide they become heavier with increase in speed, but by no more than is required to impart good "feel".

The aeroplane was dived to 380 mph A.S.I. and up to that speed the ailerons were not unduly heavy, and gave adequate response.

The ailerons are effective down to the stall and give adequate control when landing and taking off. The response is quick under all conditions of flight, and during all manoeuvres required from a fighting aeroplane.

There was no snatch or aileron vibration at any speed, and in general the aileron control is excellent for a high speed fighting aeroplane.

Rudder
On the ground the rudder control operates freely and without play. There is an excellent adjustment for the position of the rudder bar. In the air it is moderately light and extremely effective. The rudder becomes heavier with increase of speed, but by no more than is necessary in a high speed aeroplane, and at the highest speeds it is still effective.

The aeroplane responds easily and quickly to the rudder under all conditions of flight.

Although the rudder is heavier than the ailerons, yet it should not be made lighter as with a very light rudder the pilot might overload the aeroplane at high speeds.

Rudder Bias Gear
The rudder bias control was quick and easy to operate, it is effective and gives adequate range.

Elevators
On the ground full movement of the elevators can be obtained. Operation is light and there is no play.

In the air the elevator control is light and very effective down to the stall.

Heaviness increases with speed, but by no more than is necessary. In the dive the aeroplane is steady. The elevators give rapid response with a small movement of the control column. When landing the control column need not be fully back.

The control is satisfactory as regards "feel" and response, but would be improved if the movement of the control column for a given movement of the elevators was slightly greater. A small movement of the control column produces so large an effect that an unskilled pilot might pull the nose of the aeroplane up too much when landing; however, a change to alter the gearing between control column and elevator is not considered advisable until spinning trials show it to be safe.

Tail Trimming Gear
The tail trimming gear, which is of the trimmer tab type, is easy to operate and very effective. A very small movement of the lever has a powerful effect, and a lower gearing would be an advantage. There is adequate range for trim for all conditions of flight, in fact, only half the available movement of the lever is required.

Engine Controls
Engine controls are well placed in the cockpit. They work easily and without play and do not slip.

Flaps
The flaps are operated pneumatically and move down through an angle of 60°. Control is by a switch moved one way for "down" and the other way for "up". The system

worked well and gave no trouble in maintenance.

When the flaps are down they reduce the stalling speed by about 12 mph A.S.I. (Uncorrected) and the aileron control is better at the stall with the flaps down than with them up. Putting the flaps down caused a noticeable change in trim, which can easily be taken up on the trimming gear or on the elevators.

Although these flaps appreciably reduce the flatness of glide, yet this aeroplane would be easier to bring in if the flaps were made more effective either by putting the angle up to 90° or increasing their area.

Since this aeroplane was first flown at this Establishment the pilots have had experience of very high drag flaps on several aeroplanes, and they are unaminous in their opinion that higher drag flaps on the Spitfire would improve its characteristics in the approach, and make it easier for the unskilled pilot to get into a small aerodrome.

If the flaps are modified to give higher drag, two "down" positions should be provided (say 60° and 90°) because a very high drag flap, although suitable for use in day time, involves too sudden a change of attitude when flattening out during a landing at night.

The ideal system of operation is a smaller lever by which the flaps can be set to any position as required, but failing this, a system of operation to allow of two settings for the flaps at 60° and 90° is essential.

Brakes
The brakes are hand operated with differential control on the rudder. They are smooth, progressive, easy to operate and effective. They do not tend to tip the aeroplane up at the end of the landing run.

FLYING CONTROLS

Stability
Laterally the aeroplane is stable. If one wing is depressed and the control column released the aeroplane will return to a level keel in a reasonable time. Directionally the aeroplane is stable under all conditions of flight, engine on or off. Longitudinally the aeroplane is neutrally stable with engine on and stable in the glide. The aeroplane is unstable in the glide with flaps and undercarriage down.

In general the stability characteristics are satisfactory for a fighting aeroplane and give a reasonable compromise between controllability and steadiness as a gun platform.

Characteristics at the stall
As the elevator control is very powerful the aeroplane will stall long before the control column is moved right back. The stall is normal. There is no vice nor snatch on the controls. In tight turns, giving approximately 3g as registered on the accelerometer, at speeds from 140 mph A.S.I. downwards there was a distinct juddering on the whole aeroplane. Under these conditions the aeroplane is probably in a semi-stalled condition and this juddering effect may be due to slight buffeting on the tail. This can be stopped at once if the control column is eased forward.

Tests according to A.D.M. [aircraft design memorandum] 293 were done with the following results:-

On No 1 test with the undercarriage and flaps up it is difficult to keep the aeroplane steady when the control column is right back. It wallows from side to side and there is snatch on the control column from the elevators. With the undercarriage and flaps down the aeroplane is steadier in the stalled glide and there is no snatch.

In Test No 2 with the undercarriage and flaps down it was possible to pull the wing up when ailerons were applied to unbank, but in turns both to the left and to the right, the aeroplane tends to take charge at the stall and cannot be said to comply with these tests when the control column is pulled right back.

In the third test with the undercarriage and flaps up, the wing can be pulled up, but in this test again the aeroplane takes charge to such an extent that the pilot found it almost impossible to make sure of centralising the rudder. With the undercarriage and flaps down the aeroplane's behaviour was much the same.

In tests Nos 2 and 3 the movements of the aeroplane are more violent to the right than to the left after applying the controls. No spin resulted in either of these two tests.

This aeroplane, in common with other fighters tested at this Establishment, cannot be said to comply fully with tests Nos 2 and 3, as its behaviour depends so much on the way the pilot uses his controls. Its behaviour in test No 1 indicates that there is sufficient lateral control at the stall for a heavily loaded high speed aeroplane of this type.

Aerobatics
Loops, half rolls off loops, slow rolls and stall turns have been done. The aeroplane is very easy and pleasant to handle in all aerobatics.

Landing and take-off
The aeroplane is easy and normal to take-off. There is a slight tendency to swing, but this is not so pronounced as on a Fury and is automatically and easily corrected by the pilot. The aeroplane is simple and easy to land, but requires very little movement of the control column as the elevator control is so powerful, and it is not necessary to have the control column fully back.

If the engine is opened up with the flaps and undercarriage down, the aeroplane can be easily held by the control column. The aeroplane does not swing when landing.

Sideslipping
The aeroplane does not sideslip readily.

Ground handling
The ground handling is exceptionally good. The aeroplane is easy to turn and taxi in fairly strong winds. It is a more satisfactory aeroplane for operating in high winds than the normal biplane fighter.

UNDERCARRIAGE

The undercarriage has excellent shock absorbing qualities, and good rebound damping.

The controls for the hydraulically retracting mechanism are simple and well arranged. The undercarriage can be raised in about 10 seconds and lowered in about 15 seconds, without undue effort. The indicators were satisfactory. The wheels cannot be seen, but when the undercarriage is lowered two small rods project through the wings to show its position.

When the undercarriage is fully up or down, the hand lever of the oil pump can no longer be moved, and this is a useful additional indication that the undercarriage is in the required position.

A Klaxon to warn the pilot that the undercarriage is up works when the throttle is pulled back beyond two thirds, but is not loud enough to be heard by him with the cockpit open and the engine on.

FLYING VIEW

View forwards is fair and upwards is good. View to the rear is fair for a covered cockpit.

The present windscreen gives great distortion. If a curved windscreen of this shape cannot be made in either moulded glass or in suitable material to give no distortion, it is considered that it should be replaced by a flat-sided type, even though this might involve a slight reduction in performance.

With the cover open, the cockpit is remarkably free from draught, and it is possible to land and take-off with the cockpit cover open without using goggles.

COCKPIT COMFORT

The cockpit is comfortable and there is plenty of room, even for a big pilot. The head room is somewhat cramped for a tall pilot. It is not unduly noisy and the instruments and controls are well arranged. The cockpit is easy to enter and leave when the aeroplane is on the ground and foot steps on the wing are not considered necessary.

At speeds over 300 mph A.S.I. the cockpit cover is very difficult to open, although it has been opened at 320 mph A.S.I., and will stay open. Attention should be given to this question, as it is most important that the pilot should be able to get out of the aeroplane at the very highest speeds without difficulty. A small air flap operated by the handles on the sliding cover might make it easier to open at high speeds.

Although no heating is provided the cockpit was kept warm by heat from the engine and exhaust at 25,000 ft. Gloves were not necessary.

INSTRUMENTS

All instruments are well arranged and are clearly visible to the pilot. The compass is steady at all speeds.

SUMMARY OF FLYING QUALITIES

The aeroplane is simple and easy to fly and has no vices. All controls are entirely satisfactory for this type and no modification to them is required, except that the elevator control might be improved by reducing the gear ratio between the control column and elevator. The controls are well harmonised and appear to give an excellent compromise between manoeuvrability and steadiness for shooting. Take-off and landing are straightforward and easy.

The aeroplane has rather a flat glide, even when the undercarriage and flaps are down and has a considerable float if the approach is made a little too fast. This defect could be remedied by fitting higher drag flaps.

In general the handling of this aeroplane is such that it can be flown without risk by the average fully trained service fighter pilot, but there can be no doubt that it would be improved by having flaps giving a higher drag.

Appendix F.

SPECIFICATION No F.16/36
28th July 1936

Spitfire I Development and Production

This Specification covered the 310 Spitfires of the first production contract, which was signed on June 3rd 1936. The first paragraph stated:-

"The aircraft are to be constructed in strict accordance with the drawings and schedules covering the design, construction, etc., of the experimental aircraft built to Specification No F.37/34 in the form in which that aircraft is finally accepted by the Director of Technical Development as the prototype of the production aircraft, except as modified by other requirements of this Specification or by alterations accepted by the Director of Technical Development to facilitate production."

The document then went into contractual details not important to the Spitfire story, before listing in paragraph 10 the changes to the prototype aircraft which were required or permitted:

(i) Provision is to be made in the structure for such extra weight as will be entailed, should a Fairey Reed three-blade metal airscrew be fitted in place of a wooden two-blade airscrew.

(ii) Two chutes, each 30 inches long × 5¾ inches in diameter, are to be provided to enable the pilot to drop forced landing flares.

(iii) The capacity of the lower fuel tank is to be increased by 9 gallons, and space shall be reserved in one of the wings for an extra tank of 9 to 12 gallons capacity. Should the extra tank be required, a hand pump will be necessary for feeding its contents to the upper tank, on which a suitable connecting point is to be provided.

(iv) Arrangements are to be made for the safe disposal of any petrol which may leak from the tanks.

(v) The lower fuel tank is to be provided with a detachable sump.

(vi) The stiffness of the wings is to be increased so as to ensure freedom from flutter up to an indicated airspeed of 450 mph. In particular, the spar web is to be moved from front to rear of the flange and thicker leading edge sheeting is to be provided.

(vii) A tube through which the Very pistol may be fired is to be provided.

(viii) Hot and cold air intake pipes of Rolls-Royce type are to be fitted if found suitable.

(ix) A locker of dimensions not less than 14″ × 10″ × 4″ is to be provided to hold the pilot's personal belongings.

(x) A tail wheel with an electrically conducting tyre is to be fitted.

(xi) A curved windscreen is to be fitted in lieu of flat panels if a satisfactory type can be obtained sufficiently early.

(xii) The cockpit hood shall be easy to open at all speeds of which the aeroplane is capable.

(xiii) A means of regulating the temperature of the cockpit by the admission of cold air thereto is to be provided.

(xiv) At those parts of the mainplane or tailplane where riveting of the covering would be particularly difficult to do, the ribs may be made with their lower booms of wood and the covering attached by stainless steel wood screws.

(xv) The undercarriage horn is to be modified so as to give a more audible warning.

(xvi) The wing tip navigation lamps are to be of standard pattern.

(xvii) The gun firing control is to be of Dunlop pneumatic type.

(xviii) The pump which actuates the undercarriage retracting mechanism shall be modified so as to increase the speed of raising and lowering the undercarriage.

(xix) The mechanical control for rotating the undercarriage lock is to be made specially robust.

(xx) If possible, R.A.E. Type G landing lamps shall be fitted.

(xxi) Provided no reduction in the performance will be entailed, the hinged flaps on the wheels may be replaced by fixed flaps which, when retracted, will not cover the wing apertures completely.

(xxii) The wing tips and the end bay of the fuselage are to be made easily detachable. These components, together with each wing as a whole, shall comply with current interchangeability requirements.

(xxiii) The plating for the wings and fuselage may be made of Alclad, which shall be protected by varnish in accordance with the relevant A.D.M.

(xxiv) The spar tubes may be made of Hiduminium, provided all relevant requirements as regards their strength are met.

(xxv) Forgings may be of non-stainless steel, protected in accordance with current requirements.

(xxvi) The aeroplanes shall be "camouflaged". Further instructions in connection with this requirement will be issued at a later date.

(xxvii) A simple type of jack, suitable for raising the aeroplane when the undercarriage retracting mechanism has to be tested, is to be provided to "special order only".

(xxviii) The pilot's instrument board is to be arranged to take the new flying instrument panel.

(xxix) The gearing of the elevator trimming tabs is to be reduced, and back-lash at the tabs on both elevator and rudder is to be eliminated, or minimised as far as possible.

(xxx) The pipe-lines in the braking system are to be secured to the oleo legs.

(xxxi) The fairing over joints in the wing covering is to be such that cracks will not develop therein.

(xxxii) The clearance above the pilot's head is to be increased.

(xxxiii) The oil cooling is to be improved so that it will be satisfactory for English Summer conditions.

Spitfire I's of No 65 Squadron, pictured shortly before the outbreak of war. *Charles Brown*

1.

SPITFIRE OPERATIONAL TRIALS

Early in 1939 Spitfires K 9787, K 9788 and K 9793, respectively the first, second and seventh production aircraft, took part in the type's operational trials at the Royal Air Force test centre at Martlesham Heath. The report on the trials took the form of answers to a standard questionnaire. The document, excerpts of which are given below, gives a wealth of little-known information on the aircraft.

* * *

AEROPLANE AND ARMAMENT EXPERIMENTAL ESTABLISHMENT MARTLESHAM HEATH
Spitfire Nos K–9787, K–9788, K–9793 (Merlin II) Operational Trials

Is the aircraft weather-proof when pegged out in the open in average weather conditions?

Airscrew and cockpit covers are provided, these fit well and are adequate. No covers are supplied for the engine, but the cowling fits well and covers may not be necessary. This can only be shown by prolonged periods of exposure.

Are the pegging down, mooring and anchorage facilities satisfactory?

Channels are provided in the wings near the wing tip, through which ropes can be passed for securing to pickets. The tail is held down by a length of rope passed completely round the fuselage forward of the tail plane. The controls can be locked. The facilities for mooring are satisfactory.

What time is required to swing the compass with standard service facilities provided?

Compass swinging with undercarriage down can be done in about 30 minutes. No facilities for swinging the compass with undercarriage up are available.

What is the minimum time to:-
(i) refuel with standard service refuelling equipment?
A difference has been found in the balance pipes between the tanks. A larger pipe is fitted in K–9793 than in K–9788. The times to refuel from a standard 450 gallon trailer using the pump are:

K–9788   11 mins (small balance pipe)
K–9793   4 mins (large balance pipe)
(ii) re-arm with ammunition?
 30 mins—4 armourers
(iii) change oxygen cylinders?
$4\frac{1}{2}$ mins
(iv) remove and replace guns?
Remove guns—40 minutes ⎫
Replace guns—30 minutes ⎬ 4 armourers
(v) change batteries
$4\frac{1}{2}$ minutes

Can all five operations be carried out simultaneously?
No.

Is frequent change of batteries necessary?
No.

Is ammunition stowage satisfactory?
The gun bays and belt boxes are covered by 22 panels and it is necessary to undo more than 150 turn buttons when removing them. Belt boxes satisfactory.

Are flying instruments positioned and illuminated satisfactorily?
Yes.

Is manoeuvrability while taxiing satisfactory?
The aeroplane has been taxied in winds up to 30 mph. Manoeuvrability on the ground is satisfactory. Brakes are normally used and are satisfactory.

Opposite: The first production Spitfire, serial K 9787, seen shortly after its first flight in May 1938.
Charles Brown

Spitfire I, access panels.

1. Rudder tab control pulleys
2. Handhole (port only)
3. Wireless compartment (port only)
4. Engine cowling panels
5. Tail wheel unit
6. Electrical connections (port only)
7. Tail wheel shock-absorber strut
8. Accumulator stowage
9. Aileron hinges and control lever
10. Landing lamps
11. Flap operating cylinder
12. Radiator mounting
13. Radiator fairing
14. Pneumatic system charging valve
15. Pipe connections inside fairing
16. Oil cooler fairing
17. Flap operating gear
18. Handhole (starboard only)
19. Pressure head
20. Handhole
21. Mooring rope
22. Browning guns and ammunition boxes
23. Fuel drain cock
24. Coolant vent cock
25. Electrical connections
26. Browning guns

Panels shown dotted are in top surface

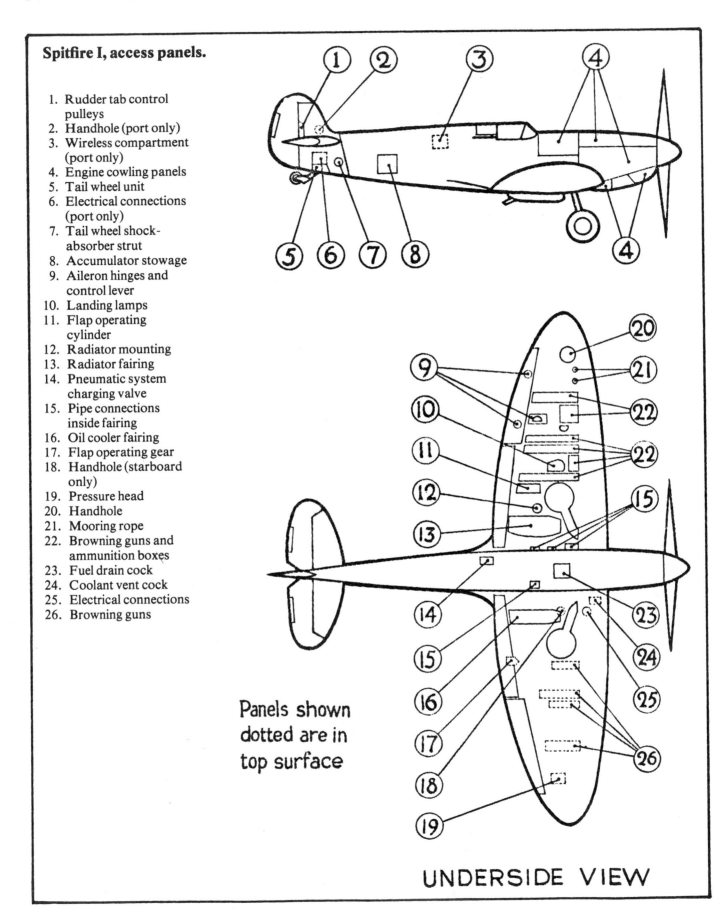

UNDERSIDE VIEW

What is the minimum size of aerodrome (grass surfaced) from which the aircraft can operate in still air?

	Wooden Airscrew	Metal Two Pitch Airscrew
Take-off run	420 yds	320 yds
Distance to 50 ft screen	720 yds	490 yds
Landing run	380 yds	235 yds
Distance from 50 ft screen	700 yds	560 yds

The minimum size of aerodrome should exceed these dimensions by about 20 per cent to allow for slope, ground softness and high air temperature.

What is the minimum time required to climb to:
30,000 ft?
Service ceiling?

	Wooden Airscrew	Metal Two Pitch Airscrew
	$22\frac{1}{2}$ mins	24 mins
	32 mins	—

What is its forward speed during this climb?

	Wooden Airscrew	Metal Two Pitch Airscrew
Climbing speed to 12,000 ft	175 mph (ASI)	192 mph (ASI)

Speed reduced 2 mph per 1,000 ft from 12,000 ft upwards.

What is the maximum speed in level flight at:-

	ASI [Indicated Air Speed]		True Air		R.P.M.	
	(a)	(b)	(a)	(b)	(a)	(b)
(i) 1,000 feet?	295	—	291	—	2335	—

Spitfire serial K9787, with Jeffrey Quill at the controls.

(ii) 10,000 feet?	292	—	328	—	2650	—
(iii) 15,000 feet?	288	—	348	—	2820	—
(iv) 20,000 feet?	276	280	361	365	2940	3000
(v) 30,000 feet?	202	—	315	—	2660	—

(a) Two bladed wooden airscrew
(b) Three bladed metal airscrew

What is the most economical cruising speed with wooden airscrew at 15,000 ft and what are the appropriate engine revolutions, mixture settings?

ASI mph	True Air Speed mph	rpm	Boost lb/sq in
198	240	2090	—4

mixture control set to automatic 'weak'

What is the fuel and oil consumption rate?
fuel	29.1 galls/hr
oil	$\frac{3}{4}$ gall/hr

To what extent is the aircraft manoeuvrable in the air at all heights and speeds under manual control?

Manoeuvrability is good throughout the speed range during climb or in level flight except that the increasing heaviness of the ailerons reduces the manoeuvrability at speeds above about 240 ASI with the original production ailerons, 340 ASI with smooth strung ailerons. In dives at speeds near 450 ASI the ailerons become almost immovable.

Limitations in Dives
Speed 450 mph ASI
1/3 Throttle or more	3600 rpm
Less than 1/3 throttle	3000 rpm

Behaviour in Dives
Aircraft is very steady in dive. Aileron and rudder controls become very heavy. If rudder bias is not correctly adjusted a slight yaw will take place which will produce a heavy wing down effect.

SPITFIRE I

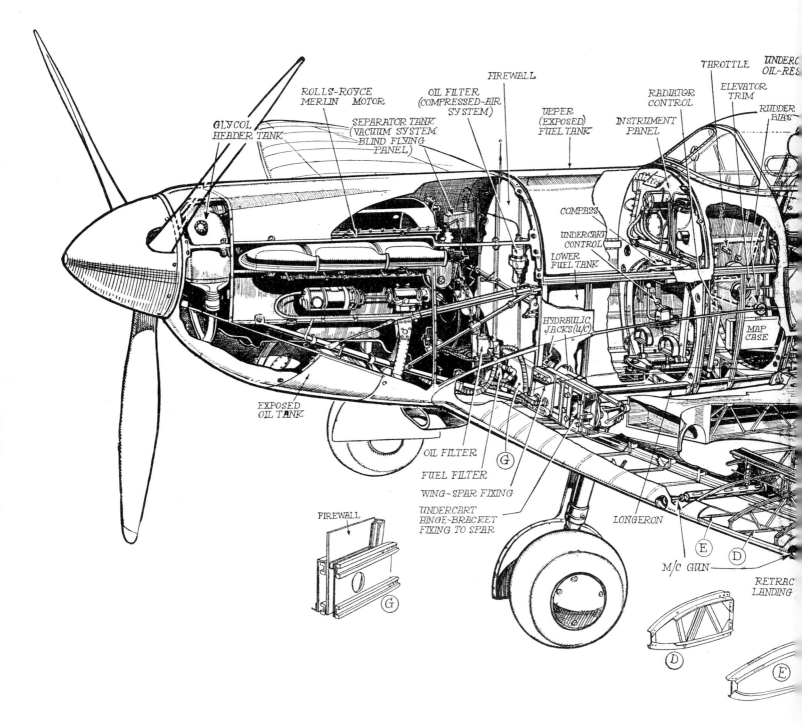

GLYCOL
HEADER TANK

ROLLS-ROYCE
MERLIN MOTOR

SEPARATOR TANK
(VACUUM SYSTEM
BLIND FLYING
PANEL)

OIL FILTER
(COMPRESSED-AIR
SYSTEM)

FIREWALL

UPPER
(EXPOSED)
FUEL TANK

RADIATOR
CONTROL

THROTTLE

ELEVATOR
TRIM

UNDERC
OIL-RES

INSTRUMENT
PANEL

RUDDER
BIAS

COMPASS

UNDERCART
CONTROL

LOWER
FUEL TANK

MAP
CASE

HYDRAULIC
JACKS (u/c)

EXPOSED
OIL TANK

OIL FILTER

FUEL FILTER

WING-SPAR FIXING

UNDERCART
HINGE-BRACKET
FIXING TO SPAR

G

LONGERON

M/C GUN

E

D

RETRAC
LANDING

FIREWALL

G

D

E

Cut-away of Mark I Spitfire of the main production batch, drawn by J.H. Clarke of 'The Aeroplane', showing several of the changes to the prototype called for in Specification F.16/36. Amongst these were: the addition of the two flare chutes and the ditty box behind the cockpit; the tail wheel in place of the original skid; a retractable landing light under the port wing; a push-out panel on the port side of the cockpit hood, to enable the pressure inside and outside to be equalised so that it could be opened at high speed; a bulged hood to increase the clearance over the pilot's head; and the removal of the hinged flaps covering the outer part of the wheels when the undercarriage was retracted. From the 78th production aircraft, the 3-bladed de Havilland metal airscrew was fitted as standard.

57

OXYGEN BOTTLE

AIR BOTTLES

DITTY BOX

PARACHUTE FLARES

RADIO

BACKBONE

FIRST-AID STOWAGE

HATCH (ST'BD)

SKIN PLATING ASSEMBLED COMPLETE WITH STRINGERS

BACKBONE END

CLARK

U/C WARNING HORN

ACCUMULATORS

LONGERONS

TAIL WHEEL SHOCK ABSORBER

GUN HEATING DUCT

FLAP

F

F

ALERON

M/C GUN

M/C GUN

9593

Above: Close-up of the bulged cockpit canopy, an early modification to provide sufficient headroom for tall pilots.

Left: The seventh production Spitfire, serial K 9793, took part in the operational trials fitted with a de Havilland metal three-bladed two-pitch airscrew which enhanced take-off performance and increased maximum speed by 4 mph. On the 78th and subsequent production aircraft, this type of propeller was fitted as standard. *Crown Copyright*

Is any undue fatigue imposed on any member of the crew during a flight to full operational range at any height due to such factors as cramped position, cold, engine noise, vibration, etc?

No fatigue is imposed due to the cramped position, engine noise, or vibration. For flights above 25,000 ft standard clothing and boots provide adequate warmth for short periods. For periods over $\frac{1}{2}$ hour some discomfort is felt due to cold hands and feet. At low heights the cockpit becomes too warm with the hood shut, this is most likely to cause fatigue flying at low heights when dressed for high flying. Fatigue would occur when flying with the hood open due to considerable cockpit draughts. To cover this condition and also for formation flying it would be advantageous if the hood could be fixed when open a small amount, say 2 or 3 inches.

Can the pilot readily abandon the aircraft by means of parachute in emergency?

The clearance for exit with parachute is limited and exit in high speed flight might be difficult. Exit would be easier from the port side, a side door being fitted. The top of the hood is difficult to slide back even with two hands at speeds in excess of 250 mph and at higher speeds there is a risk of injury to the arms in getting the hood fully back. It

Spitfires of the initial production batch undergoing final assembly at the Supermarine hangar at Eastleigh. Mechanics are seen lifting the two-bladed fixed-pitch wooden propeller, made by The Airscrew Company, into position. Specification F.16/36 required that the aircraft be able to take either the wooden propeller (weighing 83 lb) or a three-bladed metal airscrew (weighing about 350 lb). This meant that if the lighter propeller was fitted, 135 lb of lead ballast had to be carried in the nose; the oblong weights on the starboard side can be seen just beneath the forward end of the engine. The aircraft nearest the camera, the forty-fifth production Spitfire serial K 9831, did not have a distinguished career. It was delivered to No 41 Squadron at Digby on December 30th 1938 and was damaged beyond repair in an accident exactly one month later; it ended its days as a ground instructional machine at the RAF Apprentice training school at Halton. At the time this photograph was taken, early in December 1938, Spitfire production was running at about three aircraft per week. *Vickers*

is necessary for the hood to be fully back in order to open the side door.

Is the pilot's view satisfactory by day under all conditions of weather for flying formation in:-

(i) "V"   In fine weather the view is good with the hood open, but view through the Perspex is always difficult especially into the sun, and is made more so when the Perspex becomes scratched or covered with oil. In bad weather or, in cloud, it would be advisable to fly in formation with the hood open. [Obviously the Martlesham pilots had not yet got into the habit of nagging the ground crews to keep the Perspex spotlessly clean and polished]

(ii) Box?   The remarks above refer also to Box formation.

Are there any acceleration or deceleration difficulties in station keeping in formation flying by day?

None in normal flight, but acceleration and deceleration are poor [compared with biplane fighters], so that rapid manoeuvres in formation are less easy.

What is the best speed for accurate formation flying?

About 230 mph indicated.

Are there likely to be any substantial differences in fuel and oil consumption rates between aircraft cruising in formation?

Trials using two aeroplanes indicated that no considerable differences of consumption should be expected. Greater differences would probably be experienced with larger formations.

What times are required to make daily and periodical inspections?

Inspection	Airframe	Engine
Daily	$1\frac{1}{4}$ man hr	$1\frac{1}{4}$ man hr
20 hrs	$6\frac{1}{2}$ man hrs	7 man hrs
40 hrs	Not done	

Early service Spitfires.

Opposite, top: Ground running a Spitfire I of No 19 Squadron, the first unit to receive the new fighter, at Duxford. *Cozens. Opposite, centre*: Spitfire I of No 66 Squadron, the second unit to receive the type, also at Duxford. The object mounted above the starboard wing was a combat camera. *Dymond. Left, top*: Spitfire I of No 72 Squadron believed to be piloted by the commander, Squadron Leader R.A. Lees. This aircraft carries the squadron badge on the arrow-head on the fin. *72 Sqdn. Left, centre*: Corporals Griffiths and Starke of A Flight No 72 Squadron posing in front of one of the unit's Spitfires at Church Fenton. *72 Sqdn. Below*: Units of No 12 Group of Fighter Command concentrated at Digby in May 1939, prior to the last Empire Air Day on the 20th. To publicise the event the Group's squadrons made a massed fly-past over a circuit of Midland towns and cities. The Spitfires in the foreground belonged to No 19 Squadron (WZ code letters); those behind belonged to No 41 Squadron (PN code letters). *72 Sqdn*

This Spitfire I, serial K 9791, was the first to be fitted with the Rotol constant-speed propeller. Compared with the earlier two-pitch type, this reduced the take-off run by about a quarter (to 225 yards compared with 320 yards) and the time to climb to 20,000 feet by more than a third (7.7 minutes compared with 11.3 minutes). The Rotol propeller was fitted to the Spitfire in the British trials against the Messerschmitt 109E; the Spitfire in the German trials was fitted with the older two-pitch propeller. *Vickers*

The Messerschmitt 109E, which was compared with the Spitfire I during separate trials in the summer of 1940 in Britain and in Germany.

2

SPITFIRE I VERSUS MESSERSCHMITT 109E

In November 1939 the French captured intact a Messerschmitt 109E–3, the latest version of this fighter in service with the Luftwaffe. In May 1940 the aircraft was handed over to the Royal Air Force and the following month it was sent to the Royal Aircraft Establishment at Farnborough for comparative trials against the Spitfire I. The two aircraft were flown in turn by Wing Commander George Stainforth and Flight Lieutenant Robert Stanford-Tuck.

The Spitfire employed in the trials had been fitted with the Rotol constant speed propeller; at that time Fighter Command was just starting a crash programme to fit all Spitfires with this or the de Havilland constant speed propeller, in place of two-speed type. The constant speed propeller automatically adjusted the pitch angle of the blades to give the most efficient setting for the airspeed and engine revolutions selected; it further improved the take-off and climbing performance of the Spitfire, though the latter still fell short of that of the Messerschmitt.

Following the comparative flight trial, the Air Tactics Branch of the Air Ministry issued the following report in July 1940:

Comparative Trial between Me 109 and "Rotol" Spitfire
    1. The trial commenced with the two aircraft taking off together, with the Spitfire slightly behind and using +6¼ lb boost and 3,000 rpm.
    2. When fully airborne, the pilot of the Spitfire reduced his engine revolutions to 2,650 rpm and was then able to overtake and outclimb the Me 109. At 4,000 feet, the Spitfire pilot was 1,000 feet above the Me 109, from which position he was able to get on to its tail, and remain there within effective range despite all efforts of the pilot of the Me 109 to shake him off.
    3. The Spitfire then allowed the Me 109 to get on to his

tail and attempted to shake him off this he found quite easy owing to the superior manoeuvrability of his aircraft, particularly in the looping plane and at low speeds between 100 and 140 mph. By executing a steep turn just above stalling speed, he ultimately got back into a position on the tail of the Me 109.

4. Another effective form of evasion with the Spitfire was found to be a steep, climbing spiral at 120 mph, using $+6\frac{1}{4}$ lb boost and 2,650 rpm; in this manoeuvre, the Spitfire gained rapidly on the Me 109, eventually allowing the pilot to execute a half roll, on to the tail of his opponent.

5. Comparative speed trials were then carried out, and the Spitfire proved to be considerably the faster of the two, both in acceleration and and straight and level flight, without having to make use of the emergency +12 boost. During diving trials, the Spitfire pilot found that, by engaging fully coarse pitch and using —2 lb boost, his aircraft was superior to the Me 109.

The Farnborough trial proved to the satisfaction of everyone there that the Spitfire I was greatly superior to the Messerschmitt 109E—at altitudes around 4,000 feet (a similar trial showed that the two-seat Defiant was also superior to the Messerschmitt in a dogfight, which must have taken some doing!). The trouble was, however, that the German fighter pilots had no intention of dogfighting with the enemy fighters in the way the trial had suggested. It was probably the engine cooling difficulties experienced with the Messerschmitt during the Farnborough trial that concealed the fact that this aircraft could outclimb the Spitfire at almost all altitudes. The German pilots' best tactics were to climb above their foes and get into a favourable position, then dive into a high speed attack before zooming back to safety.

National pride being what it is, the reader will probably not be surprised to learn that trials carried out at about the same time at the *Luftwaffe* test centre at Rechlin with a captured Spitfire I proved to the satisfaction of everyone *there* that the Messerschmitt 109 was the superior. The Spitfire used in the trials had probably been forced down and captured during one of the air battles at the time of the Dunkirk evacuation at the beginning of June 1940. Like almost all Spitfires in front-line service at that time it was fitted with the de Havilland two-speed propeller; as a result its climbing performance was somewhat inferior to that of the Spitfire used in the Farnborough trials. The German pilots were quick to grasp the fact that the float carburetter of the Merlin engine fitted to the Spitfire ceased to deliver fuel if the pilot pushed down the nose of his aircraft and applied negative "G", with the result that the engine cut; the Messerschmitt 109 was fitted with fuel injector pumps and did not suffer from this failing.

One of the pilots who tried his hand with both the Spitfire and the Hurricane during the early summer of 1940 was *Hauptmann* Werner Moelders; with 25

Above: As well as the intact fighter version of the Spitfire the Germans also captured a reconnaissance version prior to the Battle of Britain. This PR IC, serial P 9331, belonged to the highly-secret No 212 Squadron which operated from Meaux near Paris during the spring of 1940. On June 7th it took off to photograph the battle area around Liege but suffered a glycol leak and the pilot made a forced landing at Champagne airfield near Rheims. Attempts to salvage the aircraft failed and the French authorities were asked to destroy it. The Spitfire was still intact at Champagne in September, however, when Luftwaffe *Leutnant* Diether Luckesch took this photograph. *Luckesch*

Left: The German fighter ace *Hauptmann* Werner Moelders, the top-scoring *Expert* during the first year of the war, was one of those who flew the captured Spitfire at Rechlin. As a fighting aircraft, he considered the British fighter 'miserable'.

victories over France and the Low Countries he was at that time the top-scoring fighter pilot of the Second World War. His comments are therefore worthy of note:

"It was very interesting to carry out the flight trials at Rechlin with the Spitfire and the Hurricane. Both types are very simple to fly compared with our aircraft, and childishly easy to take-off and land. The Hurricane is very good-natured and turns out well, but its performance is decidedly inferior to that of the Me 109. It has strong stick forces and is "lazy" on the ailerons.

The Spitfire is one class better. It handles well, is light on the controls, faultless in the turn and has a performance approaching that of the Me 109. As a fighting aircraft, however, it is miserable. A sudden push forward on the stick will cause the motor to cut; and because the propeller has only two pitch settings (take-off and cruise), in a rapidly changing air combat situation the motor is either overspeeding or else is not being used to the full."

Both nation's trials produced results that were valid only up to a point. The British trial had been flown at medium altitude simulating a turning fight, because there the Spitfire was the better. The German trial had been flown at high altitude simulating a high speed combat, because there the Messerschmitt was the better. When the crunch came between the Royal Air Force and the Luftwaffe, during the Battle of Britain in the late summer of 1940, most of the fighter-versus-fighter combats took place at altitudes between 13,000 and 20,000 feet because that was where the German bombers were. And in that height band the performances of the Spitfire I and the Messerschmitt 109E were rather more equal than either nation's trial had suggested; in the sort of fleeting combat that became normal between fighters, tactical initiative counted for a great deal more than the relatively minor advantages and disadvantages the two types had compared with each other.

3

SPITFIRE IN ACTION

Opposite, above: Spitfire I's of No 41 Squadron pictured during a deployment exercise early in the war, supported by Ensign transports. *Cozens*

Below: On the afternoon of June 2nd 1940 No 72 Squadron put up twelve Spitfires for an offensive patrol over the Dunkirk area. The Squadron sighted a formation of six Junkers 87 dive bombers and attacked. Flying Officer O. Pigg (in the centre of the group) made a long firing pass on one of the Junkers and saw it go down in flames. As he was breaking off, however, he came under fire from another of the German aircraft and his Spitfire was damaged. Lacking brakes, flaps and aileron control, he managed to get the aircraft back and made a wheels-up landing at Gravesend. Pigg was later killed in action, during the Battle of Britain. *72 Sqdn*

Production of Spitfire II's in full swing at Castle Bromwich in February 1941, with the 500th aircraft from the factory about to be completed. The second aircraft in the line, serial P 8076, was delivered to No 152 Squadron in March 1941. Following a nine-month service li uring which it also served with Nos 130, 411, 12   340 Squadrons, it was wrecked in an accident in December.

Above: In the early summer of 1940 Spitfires were frequently, if ineffectively, employed at night against German bombers operating over Britain. During these operations the aircraft were fitted with 'blinkers' forward of the cockpit to shield the pilot's eyes from the glare of the exhaust flames, as in the case of this aircraft of No 72 Squadron.

Right: A Spitfire of No 92 Squadron wearing the black port wing scheme used by RAF fighters between November 1940 and April 1941. *via Wood*

Opposite page, top: A Spitfire II of the Polish No 315 (Deblinski) Squadron pictured at Northolt in July 1941. In this unit the individual aircraft letters were made into girls' names, in this case Janka (Jean). *Rutkiewicz.*

Opposite page, bottom: One of the few photographs showing the Mark IB version of the Spitfire, fitted with two 20 mm Hispano cannon, in service. The aircraft depicted belonged to No 92 Squadron, which employed them in operations from Biggin Hill and Manston in the winter of 1940–1941. *92 Sqdn.*

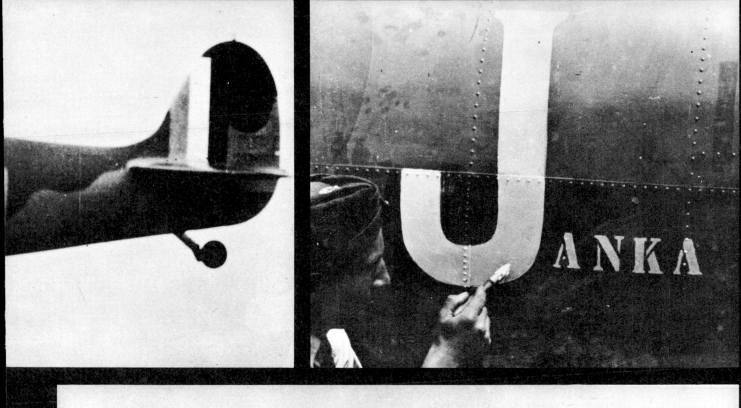

This Spitfire VB of No 403 (Canadian) Squadron was damaged when it swung out of control on landing at Horn-
church and struck a ground defensive position, in April 1942. It was repaired and put back into service.

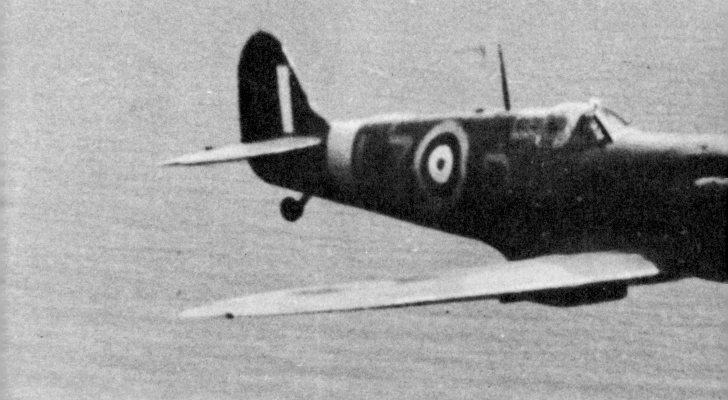

Armourers replenishing the starboard machine guns of a
Spitfire VB of No 312 (Czech) Squadron.

Right: Reconnaissance Spitfire in its element. A white-
painted Spitfire PRI 'Dicer' of the Photographic
Reconnaissance Unit seen merging against the cloud
background.

One of the few photographs showing an operational Spitfire
IIA, in this case belonging to No 66 Squadron, with a single
fixed 40-gallon fuel tank fitted to the port wing. Late in 1941
these aircraft were also issued to Nos 118 and 152
Squadrons, for operations over occupied Europe. The
asymmetric tank arrangement impaired handling, however,
and this version was not popular in service.

Reconnaissance Spitfires. *Above:* A PR IC seen near Heston in 1941, with Flying Officer S. Wise at the controls. *Left:* Close-up of the fixed port wing tank of a PR IC. In the cockpit is Flying Officer Malcolm, who later went missing during a sortie to photograph Trondheim. *Far Left:* Ground crewmen preparing a PR IC for a mission at St Eval in September 1941.

4.

SPITFIRES TO MALTA

During the first two and a half years of the war no Spitfires had operated in the fighter role from bases outside the United Kingdom. By the beginning of 1942, however, the Hurricanes and Kittyhawks which equipped the fighter squadrons in the Middle East were outclassed by the new "F" version of the Messerschmitt 109. Only the Spitfire Mark V could battle with the German fighter on equal terms at that time, and early in 1942 the first of these were sent to Malta.

Throughout 1941 the island of Malta had served as an unsinkable aircraft carrier for the bombers units which preyed on German and Italian ships carrying supplies to the armies in North Africa. Any Axis offensive in Africa had usually to be presaged by air attacks on Malta to neutralize the striking forces and allow the necessary supplies to get through. Towards the end of 1941, however, the combined German and Italian High Command in the Mediterranean decided that the time had come to put an end to the problem of Malta once and for all: the island was to be seized in a co-ordinated attack by airborne and seaborne forces.

As a preliminary to the invasion *Luftwaffe* units began moving to Sicily from the Eastern front, where the harsh Russian winter had brought a halt to large scale air operations. By the beginning of 1942 the *Luftwaffe* strength in Sicily amounted to some 200 aircraft, increasing to more than 400 by the end of March. About 190 of these were bombers, Ju 87s and Ju 88s, supported by over a hundred Messerschmitt 109F fighters. The aerial bombardment of Maltese airfields and harbour installations began in January and rapidly gathered momentum.

Point of no return. A Spitfire VB gets airborne from HMS *Eagle* on 21st March 1942 during Operation PICKET I, the second delivery of Spitfire fighters to Malta. Ahead of the pilot was a flight over a distance as great as that from London to Prague. *IWM*

The strength of the enemy air forces in Sicily meant that to send fighters to Malta by sea would have resulted in a full-scale battle, with heavy losses and no guarantee of success. Since at that time the beleaguered island was beyond the range of single-engined fighters flying from Gibraltar, there was only one way of moving them rapidly to Malta: by taking them by aircraft carrier to a point off the Algerian coast, where they were launched to fly the rest of the way. By the end of 1941 this method was well established and more than three hundred Hurricanes had been delivered to Malta in this way; in quieter times many of them had continued on to North Africa after a refuelling stop.

Early in 1942 the first Spitfires arrived in Malta after flying off the decks of aircraft carriers. During the first three such operations, in March, a total of 31 Spitfires arrived from HMS *Eagle*. From the launching point to the north of Algiers the distance to Malta by the shortest practicable route was 660 statute miles—about as far as from London to Prague. For the flight each Spitfire carried a 90 gallon slipper tank.

The Spitfires which arrived in Malta in March 1942 were too few to stem the German attack; and no more could be launched from Royal Navy carriers during the following month, as Mr Churchill explained in a personal telegram to President Roosevelt on April 1st:

"Air attack on Malta is very heavy. There are now in Sicily about 400 German and 200 Italian fighters and bombers. Malta can only now muster 20 or 30 serviceable fighters. We keep feeding Malta with Spitfires in packets of 16 loosed from EAGLE carrier from about 600 miles West of Malta.

This has worked a good many times quite well but EAGLE is now laid up for a month by defects in her steering gear. There are no Spitfires in Egypt. ARGUS is too small and too slow and moreover she has to provide the fighter cover for the carrier launching the Spitfires and for the escorting force. We would have used VICTORIOUS but unfortunately her lifts are too small for Spitfires. Therefore there will be a whole month without any Spitfire reinforcements.

2. It seems likely from extraordinary enemy concentration on Malta that they hope to exterminate our air defence in time to reinforce either Libya or their Russian offensive. This would mean that Malta would be at the best powerless to interfere with the reinforcements of armour to Rommel, and our chances of resuming against him at an early date ruined.

3. Would you be willing to allow your carrier WASP to do one of these trips provided details are satisfactorily agreed between the Naval Staffs. With her broad lifts, capacity and length, we estimate that WASP could take 50 or more Spitfires. Unless it were necessary for her to fuel WASP could proceed through the Straits at night without calling at Gibraltar until the return journey as the Spitfires would be embarked in the Clyde.

4. Thus instead of not being able to give Malta any further Spitfires during April a powerful Spitfire force could be

flown into Malta at a stroke and give us a chance of inflicting a very severe and possibly decisive check on the enemy. Operation might take place during third week of April."

Three days later the US President replied that *Wasp* would be made available to deliver fighters to Malta. She sailed into Glasgow on 10th, where she took on 47 Spitfires and their pilots; at first light on the 14th she set out for the Mediterranean.

At 06.30 hours on the morning of April 20th, at a point some 55 miles to the north of Algiers, *Wasp* turned into wind and launched first her own squadron of

fighters to cover the force, then the Spitfires. One of those who took part in the operation, code-named CALENDAR, was Pilot Officer Michael Le Bas; he now gives us the story from his viewpoint.

"In September 1941 I completed my operational training on Spitfires and was posted to No 234 Squadron at Warmwell. With that unit I took part in several fighter sweeps and escort missions over Northern France, but although we occasionally came across German fighters I personally never had the chance to fire my guns at one. At the end of March

Squadron Leader 'Jumbo' Gracie leads the first of nine Spitfires off HMS *Eagle*, during Operation PICKET I. *IWM*

1942, by which time I had the grand total of 182 flying hours on Spitfires, I suddenly received orders to join No 610 Squadron at Portreath in Cornwall which was engaged in the same type of work. No sooner did I report to the unit, however, than I learnt that "it had all been changed" and I was to go to Abbotsinch near Glasgow.

Above: Pilot Officer Michael Le Bas, whose account of the flight to Malta from USS *Wasp* appears below. *Le Bas*

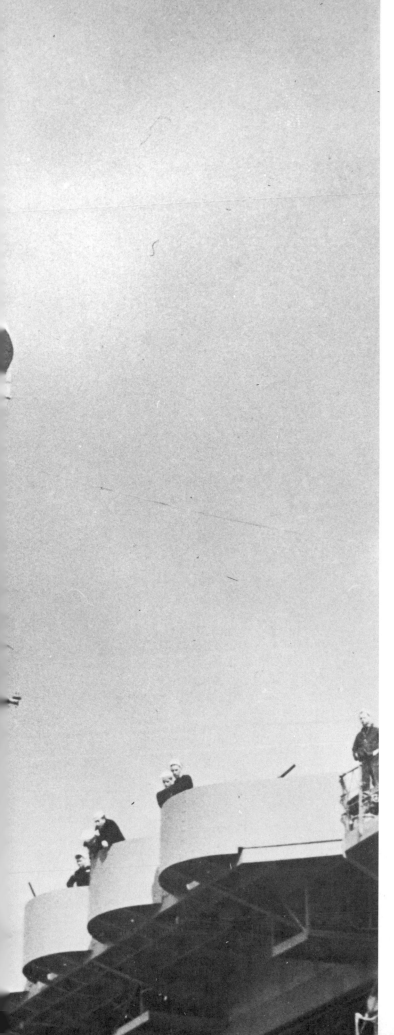

Left: A Spitfire VC, complete with four 20 mm Hispano cannon and a 90-gallon tank, being hoisted on to USS *Wasp* tied up at King George Vth Dock, Glasgow, in preparation for Operation CALENDAR in April 1942. The Spitfires had been flown into the airfields at Abbotsinch and Renfrew and moved to the dock on board 'Queen Mary' trailers. By removing the Spitfire's wing tips, it was just possible to squeeze them intact through the narrow city streets leading to the docks. *USN*

I arrived at Abbotsinch on the morning of April 12th to find that I had been allocated to No 601 Squadron under Squadron Leader John Bisdee, which was preparing to go overseas; also doing the same thing were the aircrew of No 603 Squadron. Neither squadron had any aircraft or groundcrew, but somebody had seen an American aircraft carrier docked at Glasgow and loading Spitfires. The favourite rumour was that we were to be shipped out to the Carribean to provide fighter defence against an unexpected enemy attack in that area. It turned out to be wishful thinking!

That evening the two Squadrons' aircrew boarded the carrier, the USS *Wasp*, and I had the chance to look round her. She had flown off her own aircraft except for

a single squadron of Wildcat fighters, which sat on the deck with wings folded. Below decks, the hangar was chock-full of brand new Spitfires with some of them hanging from the ceiling on straps. The aircraft were painted in unusual colours, which I later learned to be the "sand and soil" desert camouflage; each aircraft had four 20 mm cannon and carried a 90 gallon drop tank, both features I had never seen before.

The sailors made us very welcome on board *Wasp* and I shared a cabin with a US Navy Lieutenant. The evening after we boarded her *Wasp* cast off and anchored in the Clyde; early the following morning, with the battle cruiser *Renown* and six destroyers in company, we set sail for our unknown destination.

When we were well out to sea the Royal Air Force pilots were summoned to the ship's main briefing room where the force commander, Wing Commander John McLean, told us why we were there: we were to be launched from *Wasp* in a position off Algiers and fly to Malta to take part in the defence of the island. With the extra 90 gallons of fuel in the drop tank the Spitfire V had a still air range, allowing for fuel consumed in the take-off and climb, of 940 miles if the tank was carried to the destination or 1,040 miles if it was dropped when empty. Since the still air distance from the launch point to Malta would be about 660 miles, that left a fair margin in case we met unexpected headwinds or had to fight our way through enemy fighters to reach the island.

Sitting on *Wasp's* flight deck immediately after being hoisted on board, this Spitfire still has the sling in position on the forward fuselage and its wing tips in the cockpit. *USN*

The extra tank and 90 gallons of petrol, together weighing about 770 pounds, meant that the Spitfires would have to take off in the overloaded condition. There would be little margin for safety and no unnecessary weight could be carried. Two of the four cannon were to be left unloaded and the magazines of the other were loaded with only 60 rounds in each, less than half the normal complement. We were enjoined to take in our aircraft the bare minimum of personal kit and what we did carry had to be packed in such a way that the Spitfire could fight if necessary. Our bags were to be flown to Malta by courier aircraft later.

Squadron Leader "Jumbo" Gracie, who had flown to Malta from HMS *Eagle* the previous month, briefed us on the take-off from the carrier. He said the technique was to rev. up to 3,000 rpm on the brakes, then release the brakes and select emergency boost override. All of the Spitfires had taken off from the *Eagle* successfully and with the extra length of *Wasp's* flight deck getting airborne from her should be "a piece of cake". Gracie said he would lead the Spitfires off *Wasp* for this operation; after take-off the fighters were to form up in three formations of twelve and one with eleven, each formation departing when ready.

After leaving *Wasp* we were to fly along the north coast of Algeria and Tunisia as far as Cap Bon, then head south-east to skirt round the enemy-held island of Pantelleria before heading due east for Malta. McLean told us that he would be getting weather reports from Malta and we would not be launched unless clear skies were forecast over the entire route. This would be important because the only navigational equipment we carried was our maps, compasses and watches; for the final part of the flight we could get radio bearings from Malta.

The US Navy air commander then told us the procedure for take-off. During the launching operation the carrier would be committed to sailing a straight course in broad daylight within easy range of enemy air bases; so obviously the sooner we were all away after the launch began, the shorter the time *Wasp* would be exposed to enemy attack. On the afternoon before the launch the first twelve Spitfires would be taken up on the flight deck and ranged aft, to leave room in the hangar to lower the aircraft suspended from the ceiling. At first light on the 20th the carrier would turn into wind and her own squadron of Wildcat fighters would take off to provide air cover. Then Gracie would go off, followed at short intervals by the remaining Spitfires on the deck. As the last aircraft began its take-off run, the Spitfire in the hangar nearest the lift was to start its engine. The lift would then go down to pick it up and take it to the deck. As soon as possible the pilot was to taxi forwards so that the lift could go down for the next Spitfire which had, in the mean time, started its engine. The whole operation would necessarily be a complicated one and our instructions were minute and detailed. Above all else, we had to follow the deck crews' instructions implicitly.

During the days following the briefing the ships headed out into the Atlantic before turning south, giving a wide berth to the outer fringes of the Bay of Biscay which were patrolled by German aircraft. Then we headed south-eastwards and passed through the Straits of Gibraltar on the night of the 18th/19th.

On the morning of April 20th we were roused early and after a breakfast and final briefing we boarded our aircraft. My Spitfire was one of those in the hangar and as I sat in my cockpit I could hear the roar of the engines of the aircraft on the deck above as they took off. Our Spitfires were all pointing towards the bow of the ship, which meant it was difficult to see what was going on in the rear of the hangar behind us. After what seemed a long wait my squadron commander, John Bisdee, received the order to start his engine and it burst into life. I was to go off immediately after him. I remember being rather worried about getting my heavily laden Spitfire off the deck until suddenly the thought occurred to me: "Bisdee weighs a good three stone more than I do, so if he gets airborne, I'll be all right!"

By craning my neck round I saw the lift come down and Bisdee's aircraft being pushed backwards on to it; then up he went. My Spitfire was pushed backwards to where his had been and I was given the signal to start my engine. No sooner had the Merlin settled down than the lift was on its way down for me. I was pushed on to the lift and up I went. Even before the lift was fully up I received the signal to taxi forwards; the deck crewman had judged things nicely and as my Spitfire began to move forwards the lift slotted into its place in the deck. My tail wheel was hardly off it before the great slab of steel was on its way down again for the next aircraft. Bisdee's Spitfire was already airborne; he had made it! Once I was on the deck with the brakes on McLean clambered on to my wing and reached into the cockpit to check that my propeller was in fine pitch. He was checking each Spitfire before it took off; the engine had to be started with the propeller in coarse pitch and if it was left in that position the aircraft would not accelerate quickly enough to gain anything like flying speed before it reached the end of the deck. When McLean was satisfied he jumped off my wing, the deck officer began rotating his checkered flag and I pushed forwards my throttle until I had maximum rpm. His flag then fell and I released the brakes and pushed the throttle to emergency override to get the last ounce of power out of my Merlin. The Spitfire picked up speed rapidly in its headlong charge down the deck, but not rapidly enough. The ship's bows got closer and closer and still I had insufficient airspeed and suddenly—I was off the end. With only 60 feet to play with before I hit the water, I immediately retracted the undercarriage and eased forward on the stick to build up my speed. Down and down with the Spitfire until, about fifteen feet above the waves, it reached flying speed and I was able to level out. After what seemed an age but was in fact only a few seconds, my speed built up further and I was able to climb away. Nobody had told me about that at the briefing! It had been a hairy introduction to flying off an aircraft carrier; things had happened so quickly that there was no time to think. Perhaps it was just as well.

Once I had a bit of height I switched to the fuel in the drop tank and was relieved that my engine continued running, which showed that the tank was feeding properly. For the launch *Wasp* had been heading south-westwards into the 15 mph wind. High above and in front of me Bisdee took his aircraft in a wide orbit round the carrier so that I and the pilots behind me could get into position in formation as rapidly as possible. Once we had formed up, the twelve Spitfires turned due east for our new home.

When at our cruising altitude of 10,000 feet we throttled back to 2,050 rpm to get the most out of each gallon of fuel. At first the skies were clear of cloud and to the south of us we could make out the reddish-brown peaks of the mountain range which ran along the Algerian coast. As we settled down for the long flight

boredom began to set in and I remember being worried in case I lost concentration and would not be alert enough if we came under attack.

The sun climbed higher and higher in front of us, disconcertingly bright. At the same time the ground haze gradually thickened until it swallowed up the mountains which had provided a useful check on our navigation. Now there was no alternative but to continue on our compass heading, comforted only by the even drone of our Merlin engines.

Things were to get worse before they got better. As we continued eastwards cloud began to build up beneath us, hiding the sea and our important turning point at Cap Bon. About half an hour before we were due to reach Malta we expected to be in VHF range, so Bisdee broke radio silence and called up for a homing. After a short pause a voice came up in good English and gave us a north-easterly heading to fly. Had we followed the instructions we should have been in trouble but, by a stroke of good luck, the cloud beneath us started to break up and we could see the sea again. Out to port was the Italian-held island of Pantelleria, which gave us a useful navigational fix; it was clear that the homing instructions had come from an enemy station and we ignored them. Bisdee led us in a turn to the south-east, to regain our proper track.

Just as were passing Pantelleria I nearly had my own personal disaster. Without warning, my engine suddenly cut out. I thought "Oh God, this is it!" and decided that if I could not get it re-started I would glide over to the island and bale out. I jettisoned the drop tank to clean up the aircraft for the glide, then it occured to me that perhaps the tank had run dry. So I switched over to my almost-full main tank and to my great relief the engine re-started without any difficulty. I opened the throttle and regained my place in the formation.

After Pantelleria the skies cleared up completely. My first sight of Malta was the cloud of dust towering over the island after the morning visit by the *Luftwaffe*. Now my great worry was that after three hours in our cramped cockpits, stiff and with sore backsides, we should not be in good shape if we had to fight our way in. Fortunately for us, however, the Germans had gone home by the time we got there and we had no trouble getting down. Our squadron, No 601, landed at Luqa and No 603, coming up behind, landed at Takali a few miles to the west.

After landing I was directed to one of the many blast pens scattered round the airfield. I taxi-ed in and shut down my engine and almost immediately the ground crew began the slow process of refuelling the Spitfire by hand using twenty-one four-gallon petrol tins.

Of the forty-seven Spitfires which had taken off from *Wasp*, forty-six landed safely in Malta; the remaining aircraft, flown by a Sergeant pilot of No 603 Squadron, was lost without trace.

The Germans had watched our arrival on radar and that afternoon all Hell broke loose over the Maltese airfields. In spite of strenuous efforts by the fighters and the anti-aircraft gun defences, the Ju 87 and Ju 88 dive bombers and the strafing Messerschmitts managed to damage and destroy several of the newly-delivered Spitfires on the ground. The blast pens were made of local stone or stacks of petrol tins filled with sand and they provided useful protection against cannon shells and blast from anything but a direct hit. They had no roof, however, and several aircraft received damage when rocks blown high into the air by exploding bombs fell on them from above.

Since every single-engined fighter delivered to Malta for over a year had been flown in, there was no shortage of pilots for the few Spitfires available for operations at any time. As a result I did not make my first operational sortie from the island until April 24th, four days after my arrival. Led by Flight Lieutenant "Laddie" Lucas, three of us were scrambled and told to climb to 20,000 feet to engage an incoming formation of Ju 87s escorted by Messerschmitt 109s. Almost from the beginning things began to go wrong. Lucas had engine trouble and had to turn back. Then the controller took us up too high with the result that when we dived to attack we came in much too fast and two of us overshot the dive bombers. The third pilot managed to get in a good burst at a Ju 87 but then a hoard of escorting Messerschmitts got on to us and we were lucky to escape with our lives.

By the end of April the enemy attacks on our airfields had destroyed so many aircraft that there were only about half a dozen serviceable fighters on the island. Things got so bad that when enemy formations were reported coming in, those fighters which were flyable but unfit for action (for example with unserviceable guns or radios) would be ordered to scramble and orbit to the south of Malta until the raiders had gone.

There were a lot of anti-aircraft guns positioned to

Above, left: The flight deck of USS *Wasp* at dusk on April 19th 1942. Ranged ready to take-off at first light the next morning were the Wildcat fighters of USN Squadron VF-71 which were to provide air cover during the launching, then the Spitfires of No 601 Squadron. During their time on *Wasp* the Spitfires received unofficial side identification letters: No 601 Squadron's aircraft were given the number '1' followed by a letter, No 603 Squadron's aircraft were given the number '2' followed by a letter. Visible on deck are aircraft 1C, 1D 1G, 1H and 1K. The Spitfire at the head of the queue was to be flown off *Wasp* by Squadron Leader Gracie. *USN*

Below, left: Indicative of the slick timing of the take-off from *Wasp* on the morning of April 20th. Aircraft 2B of No 603 Squadron is seen about to begin its take-off run. The lift is seen on its way down for the next aircraft, which already has its engine running in the hangar. The aircraft ahead may be seen climbing away, just above the Spitfire's starboard wing tip. *USN*

90

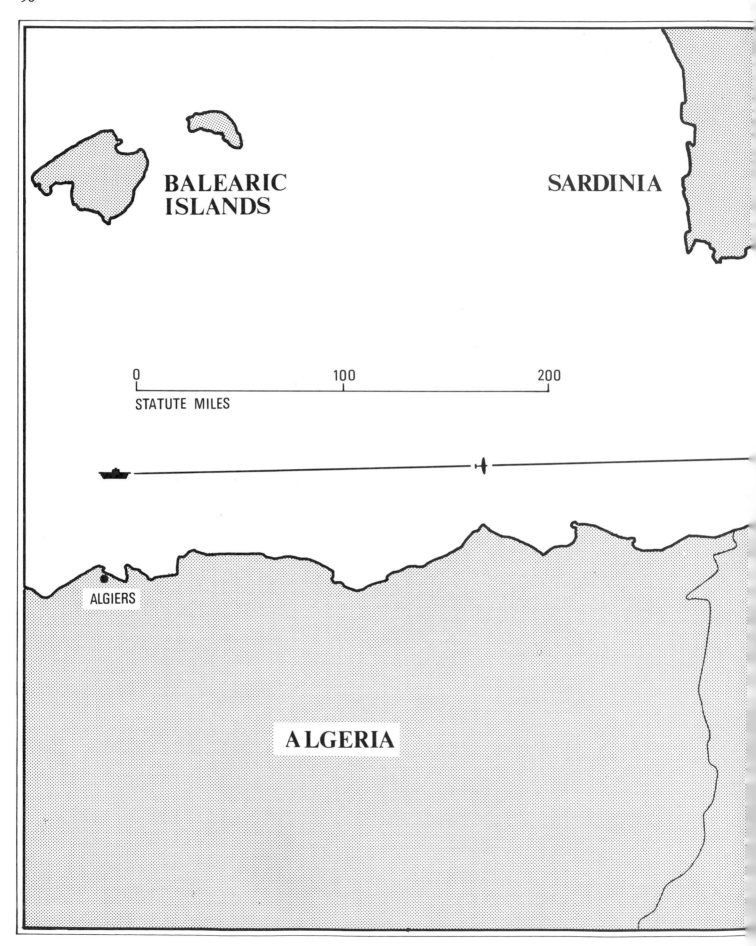

BALEARIC
ISLANDS

SARDINIA

0   100   200

STATUTE MILES

ALGIERS

ALGERIA

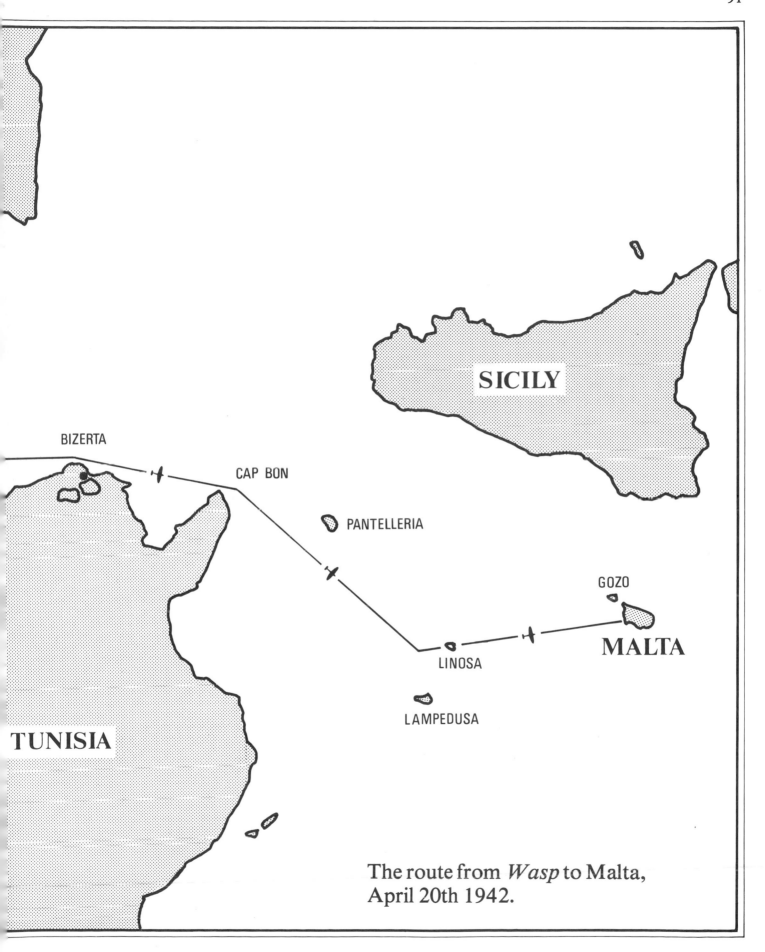

SICILY

BIZERTA

CAP BON

PANTELLERIA

GOZO

MALTA

LINOSA

LAMPEDUSA

TUNISIA

The route from *Wasp* to Malta,
April 20th 1942.

Ground crewmen and soldiers refuelling a Spitfire VC of No 601 Squadron, in a sandbagged pen at Luqa. Due to the shortage of refuelling bowsers the aircraft had to be re-fuelled using four-gallon petrol tins, twenty-one of them. This Spitfire still has its four 20 mm cannon fitted; these would not last long. Seen sitting in the cockpit is Flight Lieutenant Dennis Barnham, who later wrote the book 'One Man's Window' on his experiences in Malta; to his right, wearing a Mae West, is Michael Le Bas. *IWM*

cover the airfields and Valetta harbour; but ammunition was short and usually the gunners were rationed to a few rounds for each engagement. At irregular intervals, however, the restrictions were lifted and the gunners were allowed to put up a fine display to show the German dive bomber pilots that the defences were still in business.

I did not get my second operational sortie from Malta until May 9th, when we learned that a further large reinforcement of Spitfires was on its way in. One of the problems when I had arrived was that the operation had

been kept so secret that too few people had been told we were coming; the Spitfires had not been refuelled and rearmed quickly enough, with the result they could not take off to meet the attacks and several were knocked out on the ground. This time we were much better organised. As each Spitfire came in it was picked up at the end of the runway by a resident Malta pilot, who sat on the wing and guided the aircraft to its blast pen. At each pen there were waiting an RAF ground crew and some soldiers to help with the refuelling. I guided one Spitfire in and, even before the pilot had shut down, men were clambering on to the wings to load the cannon with their full complement of ammunition and the soldiers had started a human chain to pass up the petrol tins. The pilot pulled off his helmet and shouted to me "That's jolly good. Where's the war?" I told him "The war hasn't started for you yet, mate. Get out and be quick about it!" Within fifteen minutes of landing the Spitfire was ready to fight and shortly afterwards I received the order to scramble. Operating with No 126 Squadron I took part in the interception of a formation of Italian CANT bombers escorted by Macchi 202 fighters; three

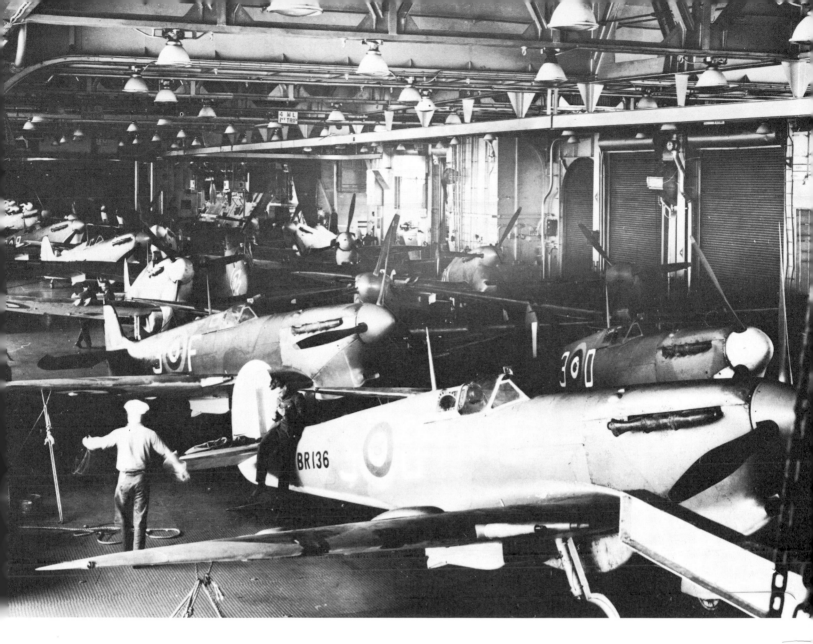

of the latter and two of the former were shot down.

The arrival of the Spitfires on May 9th, sixty of them from the carriers HMS *Eagle* and USS *Wasp*, marked a great turning point in the Battle of Malta. Before that, the fighter force had been hard put to it merely to survive in the face of the almost incessant enemy attacks. After that date the fighter squadrons were able to hit back hard and never looked back. Once there was an adequate fighter defence for the Maltese airfields the bombers and torpedo bombers could move in. The whole point of hanging on to Malta was to provide a base so that these aircraft could strike at the German and Italian ships carrying supplies to their armies in North Africa.

The Spitfires delivered during March and April had all been painted in brown and yellow desert camouflage.

This was all right when flying over land in that part of the world, but Malta was so small that we spent most of our time over the sea and in those colours the Spitfires showed up beautifully. As a result there were a lot of locally improvised paint schemes to make the aircraft less conspicuous; later reinforcement Spitfires arrived wearing the grey and green sea camouflage.

The Spitfires which had been launched from USS *Wasp* during April and May were all of the Mark VC version and were fitted with four 20mm cannon instead of the usual two cannon and four machines guns. Operating from Malta, however, this armament soon revealed its drawbacks. On the island there was a shortage of 20mm ammunition, so much so that cannon tests were prohibited; the weapons were to be fired only at the enemy. Dust was always a problem, and four cannon were twice as difficult to keep serviceable as two cannon; moreover the weight of the two extra cannon imposed a performance penalty, especially in the climb. But the greatest thing to be said against the extra two cannon was that they were unnecessary: even against the Junkers 88, the toughest bomber we had to deal

Scene from *Wasp's* flight deck on the morning of May 9th. With HMS *Eagle* in company, also laden with Spitfires, the American carrier approaches the flying-off point for BOWERY. *USN*

with, two Hispanos were quite enough. The extra two cannon were soon removed from the aircraft.

After the arrival of the Spitfires on May 9th, I was on operations or on stand-by almost every day. We remained at readiness from dawn to dusk waiting for the enemy to come to us; if they did not we stayed on the ground and it was the luck of the draw whether one did three scrambles a day or none at all. If one did recieve the order to scramble, getting off the ground was always a bit of an adventure. Because of the general shortage of equipment, the scramble order had to be given by means of Very lights fired from the control tower. For example, two reds might mean that Red Section was to scramble and two greens after that might mean that Blue Section was to take-off as well; if further sections had to scramble, things got complicated. At each blast pen someone had to be watching the control tower the whole time, because if a Very light was missed one could get in a muddle and either take-off at the wrong time or not at all. After the start up there was always a long run from one's dispersed blast pen, along the taxi way, to the end

of the runway. This was made with an airman sitting on the wing, whose job it was to guide the pilot round any new bomb craters that had appeared. Immediately one reached the runway one took off; it was always much safer in the air. After take-off the fighters would orbit the airfield until the section or squadron had formed up. Once we were airborne we could get our orders from the ground controller. He usually told us to go to the south and climb to a given altitude, then he would bring us in to engage the enemy.

After the reinforcement on May 9th, Spitfires continued to arrive on the island from aircraft carriers. Seventeen arrived on the 18th, twenty-seven on June 3rd and thirty-two on June 9th. By the middle of June things were a lot quieter over Malta, but things were going badly in Libya. The German armour had outflanked the Gazala line and on June 21st Tobruk fell. At that time there was only one Spitfire squadron, No 145, in the Western Desert and the Messerschmitt 109Fs were having an easy time against the slower Hurricanes and Kittyhawks. So on June 23rd I flew one of eight Spitfires of "A" flight of No 601 to Landing Ground 07 near Mersa Matruh in Egypt. For the flight the Spitfires were again fitted with 90 gallon drop tanks. The formation was accompanied by a Beaufighter whose crew did the

The Spitfires flown to Malta from USS *Wasp* were all of the Mark VC version, with four 20 mm cannon. Soon after their arrival, however, these aircraft had two cannon removed. In the case of this Spitfire, the two inner cannon had been taken out. *Fellows*

navigation and the flight took four and a half hours, covering about 800 miles.

"With that flight my part in the Battle of Malta ended. When we arrived in the Western Desert we pilots who had taken part in the defence of the island tended to stick together. I can imagine we got on a lot of peoples' nerves, going on all the time about the desperate conditions during the siege. We proudly wore on our battledress little Maltese crosses, carved out of shilling pieces, until a very senior officer ordered us to remove them. Looking back, the thing that strikes me is the tremendous spirit that existed amongst the fighter pilots during the siege of Malta. It simply never occured to us that we might possibly fail and that the island might fall."

●

As the summer wore on the British forces were pushed back further and further into Egypt. Mersa Matruh fell and no more Spitfires could be "exported" from Malta during 1942. In July and August there were four further re-supply operations during which a total of 125 Spitfires reached the island. These would be sufficient to enable the Malta fighter squadrons to go over to the offensive and begin mounting sweeps over Sicily.

On the day after Operation BARITONE, the re-supply operation on August 17th, the Air Ministry in London sent the following signal to the air commander at Gibraltar and to Air Vice-Marshal Keith Park, the new air commander in Malta:

"Now that Baritone is completed it is intended to dispense with further carrier operations for these reinforcements and to make deliveries of Spitfires from Gibraltar to Malta by air carrying 170 gallon jettisonable tanks. Still air range is 1380 land miles and therefore you will have to restrict dispatches to days of favourable winds on the route or at the worst to days of average still air. Under these conditions the risk of occasionally failing to reach Malta and having to land in Tunisia is acceptable. It is considered that flights by single Spitfires are likely to give better results than formations led by T.E. aircraft. Spitfire with full 170 gallon tank is slightly overloaded even without guns or ammunition but the carrying of Brownings and 200 rounds per gun is permissible and consequent reduction in range is negligible. You will therefore have to decide in consultation with Malta and taking into account the smoothness of the Gibraltar runway whether this light armament is essential or whether aircraft should proceed unarmed. Cannons and Brownings will be flown from Gibraltar to Malta by shuttle service as required. Technical instructions on fitting and use of 170 gallon tanks and on performance of aircraft so loaded follow separately. Certain additional training in navigation and in fuel economy is being carried out at home by 12 pilots out of the next batch of 32 but you should give them instruction at Gibraltar on petrol system of 170 gallon tanks and on most economical cruising speeds with that tank. The remainder of pilots should be flown in to Malta by shuttle service. Only one take off, ie that for the delivery flight, is advisable when carrying the full 170 gallon tank, and in fact any non-essential flying with the tank even empty should be avoided as these tanks are easily damaged. Commencement of these delivery flights from Gibraltar to Malta is to await instructions from Air Ministry."

Some of the previous delivery flights by Spitfires over the Mediterranean had been impressive enough, but the new reinforcement method called for flights appreciably longer: the flight from Gibraltar to Malta would take the Spitfires over a distance equal to that from London to Leningrad. On the following day Park replied:

"Considered advisable for Spitfires carrying 170 gallon petrol tanks to be fitted with two Brownings and 350 rounds per gun but not to carry cannons. Better for Spitfires to proceed in pairs instead of singly or in big formations. Not requiring any reinforcements of Spitfires

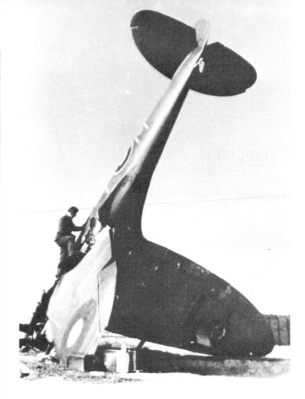

Opposite, top: A Spitfire VB of No 1435 Squadron standing in a revetment made of sand-filled petrol tins, at Luqa. This unit was formed by the expansion of No 1435 Flight into a squadron when spare aircraft and pilots became available on the island, in August 1942. *Hows*

Opposite, below: Spitfire V's of No 249 Squadron at Takali, late in 1942.

Above and below: Several Spitfires were wrecked on the ground on Malta during the German attacks. This aircraft of No 249 Squadron was wrecked by bomb blast at Takali in October 1942. *Stephens*

Believed to be the first photograph ever published showing a modified Spitfire VB fighter about to take-off from North Front, Gibraltar, for the direct flight to Malta—a distance equivalent to that from London to Leningrad. The armament had been removed, except for two .303-in machine guns. The bulge under the nose covered the extra oil tank; there was a 170 gallon fuel tank under the fuselage and a 29 gallon tank in the fuselage behind the pilot's seat. The aircraft did not carry a tropical filter for the carburetter air; this was to be fitted when it arrived in Malta. *RAF Museum*

until about second week in September."

The trials with the Spitfire fitted with the 170 gallon tank, carried out at Boscombe Down, revealed that the original estimates of fuel consumption had been optimistic. On September 5th Park was informed:

"The trials of the Spitfire V with the 170 gallon tank are now complete. Range is somewhat short for reasonable safety between Gibraltar and Malta and consequently 30 gallon internal tank is also being provided. The 170 gallon and 30 gallon tanks together with extra oil tank and necessary accessories are expected to begin arriving in Gibraltar during the first week in October. Precise date of commencement of despatch of aircraft and also rate of despatch are dependant on situation generally."

By Maltese standards, September and the early part of October 1942 had been relatively quiet. Following a run of successes by the island's anti-shipping units, however, the *Luftwaffe* returned in force. During a series of hard fought actions there were losses on both sides. On October 16th Park informed the Air Ministry:

"For the last important operation Pedestal [the supply convoy in August 1942] Malta's Spitfire strength was 163 of which 120 were serviceable. When the present battle began October 10 we had 141 Spitfires of which 113 were serviceable. The last 5 days' intensive fighting has reduced total strength to 119 of which 55 are serviceable. In addition to the absolute losses of 22 Spitfires in the last 5 days a further 20 are beyond our capacity to repair before the end of October making a total wastage of 42. If the enemy maintains his present scale of attack for another week we shall not be in a position to put up any effective fighter defence owing to lack of serviceable Spitfires. Therefore the 12 Spitfires promised by the end of October are totally inadequate as previously reported. The foregoing figures do not take into account our losses of aircraft on the ground which have been negligible but will increase in proportion as our fighter effort decreases."

Still the first Spitfires were not ready to make the direct flight from Gibraltar to Malta. So to make good the losses one last carrier reinforcement operation, TRAIN, was mounted on October 24th and 29 more Spitfires arrived on the island from HMS *Furious*. This brought the Spitfire strength on Malta to 123 aircraft of which 80 were serviceable; and even before the additional fighters arrived, the final large-scale bom-

bardment of the island by the *Luftwaffe* had petered out.

On the day following TRAIN, October 25th, the first two Spitfire fighters arrived in Malta after flying direct from Gibraltar. The Air Ministry was told:

"First 2 Spitfires with 170 gallon tanks reached Malta $5\frac{1}{4}$ hours flying. On landing both had 13 gallons oil and 43 and 47 gallons petrol respectively. Long range tanks were not jettisoned and have been returned with extra oil tanks by Liberator. 5 more Spitfires awaiting favourable weather for despatch. Briefing of these regarding engine control only required slight modification as result of experience gained in first flight. Take off presented no difficulty and run was under 800 yards."

During November and first week in December fifteen Spitfires took off from Gibraltar bound for Malta; all except one arrived safely. The flights could have con-

Date	Name of Operation	Aircraft Carriers	Aircraft Launched	Aircraft Arrived
March 7th	SPOTTER	*Eagle*	15	15
March 21st	PICKET I	*Eagle*	9	9
March 29th	PICKET II	*Eagle*	7	7
April 20th	CALENDAR	*Wasp*	47	46
May 9th	BOWERY	*Wasp* *Eagle*	64	60
May 18th	L.B.	*Eagle*	17	17
June 3rd	STYLE	*Eagle*	31	27
June 9th	SALIENT	*Eagle*	32	32
July 16th	PINPOINT	*Eagle*	32	31
July 21st	INSECT	*Eagle*	30	28
August 11th	BELLOWS	*Furious*	38	37
August 17th	BARITONE	*Furious*	32	29
October 24th	TRAIN	*Furious*	31	29
			385	367

During the operations a total of 385 aircraft were launched, of which 367 reached Malta and 18 failed to do so. The heaviest proportional loss was during Operation STYLE on June 3rd, when Messerschmitt 109's sent to Pantelleria for the purpose intercepted the incoming Spitfires and shot down four of them. The great majority of Spitfires which failed to complete the flight to Malta were lost, though this was not invariably the case. After taking-off for Operation BOWERY a Canadian, Pilot Officer Smith, found that his drop tank was not feeding properly. In accordance with the instructions given to him at the briefing, Smith jettisoned the tank and orbited the carriers until the launch was complete. Then, following the signals from *Wasp's* Deck Landing Officer, he set down the Spitfire on the carrier's deck; it was a commendable feat, since his aircraft had no arrester hook and he had no deck-landing experience. The following day, as *Wasp* was about to leave the Mediterranean, Smith again took off and landed the Spitfire at Gibraltar.

tinued but now there was no longer any urgency to supply fighters for the defence of the island. The victory at El Alamein and the subsequent German retreat meant that the siege of the island could be lifted. Never again would Malta come under serious threat from the enemy.

Above, below and opposite: The Junkers 86R high altitude bomber, used to attack targets in southern England from altitudes over 40,000 feet during August and September 1942.

5

BATTLE IN THE STRATOSPHERE

Shortly before the outbreak of war the German Junkers company had begun work on the Junkers 86P, a high altitude reconnaissance aircraft developed from the obsolescent Ju 86 bomber. In fact the new reconnaissance variant bore little resemblance to the earlier bomber: the open gun positions were faired over; there was a pressure cabin for the two-man crew; extra panels fitted to the outer wings increased the span by just under ten feet to 84 feet; and turbo-superchargers fitted to the two Jumo compression-ignition diesel engines improved the aircraft's high altitude performance. With these changes the Junkers 86P was able to cruise at altitudes around 40,000 feet, beyond the reach of fighters during the early part of the war.

The first Junkers 86P was delivered to the Luftwaffe in the summer of 1940, and during the latter half of the year the type operated at irregular intervals over the British Isles on high altitude reconnaissance missions. At that time the British radar chain was unable to track such high-flying aircraft once they had crossed the coast, and the flights went almost unnoticed by the defences. In the winter of 1940–1941 the Ju 86P was used in clandestine missions high over the Soviet Union, as part of the reconnaissance effort in preparation for the German invasion in June 1941; these flights continued after the campaign began.

In May 1942 a few Junkers 86s were delivered to the 2. *Staffel* of Long Range Reconnaissance *Gruppe 123*, based at Kastelli on Crete, from where they flew high altitude reconnaissance missions over the Cairo and Alexandria areas. These flights continued unhindered until August 24th, when Flying Officer G. Reynolds flying a stripped-down Spitfire V armed with two .5-in machine guns succeeded in intercepting one of the Ju 86s. He scored hits on the starboard engine and set it on

fire; the Junkers dived away and he lost it. There is some evidence that this was the action in which the commander of 2. *Staffel, Hauptmann* Bayer, was shot down into the sea; he and his observer ditched in their Ju 86 and were later rescued by seaplane.

Some accounts have stated that Reynolds had taken his Spitfire V up to 42,000 feet to engage the Junkers; others have spoken of later interceptions of Ju 86s by Spitfire Vs in the same area at 45,000 feet and even 50,000 feet. After a careful examination of the available evidence the author is inclined to disregard reports of Spitfire Vs intercepting enemy aircraft at altitudes much above 40,000 feet: no matter how many pieces had been taken off to lighten the aircraft, a Merlin engine with single-stage supercharging would not have developed enough power to enable a Spitfire to manoeuvre at such an altitude; moreover, above 45,000 feet, a pilot in an unpressurised cabin even breathing pure oxygen would have suffered such severe physiological problems that he could have achieved little. The interceptions of the Junkers 86s did take place, but it is probable that the German aircraft were flying at or below 40,000 feet. An explanation for the excessive altitudes stated, if they did indeed come from the pilots, could be altimeter errors or mis-readings by pilots suffering from a measure of oxygen starvation.

In the spring of 1942 the R version of the Junkers 86 appeared. This was a P version modified at the factory to have its wing span further extended, this time by more than 20 feet to almost 105 feet, and with slightly more powerful diesel engines with nitrous oxide (laughing gas) injection to increase the high altitude performance still further. As a result of these improvements the Junkers 86R was able to reach altitudes of over 45,000 feet.

During the early months of 1942 the Royal Air Force bombing attacks on Germany had begun to bite and there were persistant demands from the Nazi leadership for retaliatory attacks on Britain by the *Luftwaffe*. With the main part of the German bomber the force tied down in support of the army in the Soviet Union, however, there was little to spare for a renewed *Blitz* on Britain. The few bomber units remaining in the west did their best, but in the face of the continually strengthening British defences their attacks were costly and achieved little. So, to strengthen the force attacking England, a few Junkers 86Rs were converted into high altitude bombers. In this role the aircraft could carry only a single 550 pound bomb; but it was judged that such attacks would serve a useful propaganda purpose if they demonstrated that German bombers could operate over Britain by day with impunity.

During the third week in August 1942 two Junkers 86Rs arrived at Beauvais in northern France; the *Höhenkampfkommando* (High Altitude Bomber Detachment) began final preparations for a series of stratospheric bombing attacks on Britain. By the morning of August 24th all was ready and *Oberfeldwebel* Horst Goetz took off for the first of these operations; flying as observer in the aircraft was *Leutnant* Erich Sommer, the commander of the unit. For the first hour of the flight the Junkers remained over France, climbing steadily. Only when the bomber had reached 39,000 feet did Goetz turn north and, still climbing, head towards his target. The Ju 86R crossed the coast near Selsey Bill, dropped its single bomb on Camberley (the intended target was Aldershot), and left via Brighton having spent thirty-five minutes over Britain without interference from the defences. Shortly afterwards, the other Ju 86R attacked Southampton. Fighter Command sent up fifteen Spitfire Vs to intercept the raiders, but without success. A pair of Spitfires of the Polish-manned No 309 Squadron were directed on to Goetz's Junkers; the pilots reported that the intruder was flying at 38,000 feet and "identified" it as a Dornier 217, a type which was a more frequent visitor over Britain and which also had two engines and twin fins. Because the wing of the Junkers was nearly twice as long as that of the Dornier, the fighter pilots had mis-judged the range and thought themselves closer to the bomber than was in fact the case.

That evening the German Propaganda Ministry jubilantly announced that the *Höhenkampfkommando* had carried out the first of its daylight revenge attacks on Britain; all aircraft had returned safely. There was no hint that the grandiosely-titled unit operated but two aircraft.

On the following day, August 25th, Goetz and Sommer were again over Britain. This time, more con-fident of their immunity from interception, they flew a meandering course which took them over Southampton,

Swindon, round the north of London to Stanstead where they released their bomb, down the eastern side of the capital and crossed the coast near Shoreham. The bomber spent more than an hour over Britain, the inten-tion being to sound as many sirens as possible and cause the maximum disruption. The British authorities refused to play this game, however: single intruders were treated as reconnaissance aircraft without bombs. The sirens remained silent. Nine Spitfire Vs were scrambled to engage but none was able to get close to the bomber, which was again "identified" as a Dornier 217. From their vantage point Goetz and Sommer watched as interested spectators while the fighters zig-zagged, attempting to gain altitude without overshooting the bomber; one by one the Spitfires broke off the chase.

On the morning of the 28th one of the Junkers 86Rs attacked Bristol. The policy of not sounding the sirens for single intruders had been a calculated risk, justifiable in wartime. But on this occasion the citizens of Bristol

had to pay the penalty. The bomb landed on Broad Weir, almost in the centre of the city, during the morning rush hour. It exploded close to three buses, wrecking all of them and killing most of the people on board. It was the worst single bomb incident suffered by Bristol during the war and resulted in 48 people killed, 26 seriously injured and 30 slightly injured. During the following ten days the high-flying Junkers 86s carried out eight further attacks.

At this time the Mark VI high altitude version of the Spitfire equipped Nos 124 and 616 Squadrons of Fighter Command. This version was fitted with extended wing tips which increased the span by 3 feet 7 inches and for the pilot there was a partial pressure cabin; with these additions the Mark VI weighed 180 pounds more than the Mark V. Like the earlier version, however, the Mark VI was fitted with a Merlin with single-stage supercharging and so could not intercept anything flying above 40,000 feet. On August 29th a

The Spitfire IX, serial BF 273, flown by Pilot Officer Prince Emanuel Galitzine when he intercepted Goetz and Sommer in the Junkers 86R on September 12th 1942. The aircraft is seen prior to its modification for the high altitude role.

pair of Mark VIs of No 124 Squadron climbed to 37,000 feet but were unable to get within three miles of the Junkers 86R cruising above them.

The Mark IX version of the Spitfire, which had just entered service with Fighter Command, was fitted with the new Merlin 61 engine; and that did have a two-stage supercharger. With this refinement, the Merlin delivered 600 horse power at 40,000 feet, substantially more than was possible at such an altitude from earlier types with single-stage supercharging. To combat the high-altitude Junkers 86s a special unit was formed with modified Mark IXs. One of the pilots selected for it was Pilot Officer Prince Emanuel Galitzine who had been born in

Russia in 1918, brought to England the following year and who had lived here since. He now gives us his recollections of the operations to combat the high-flying German bombers.

●

"At the end of August 1942 I was flying Spitfire IXs with No 611 Squadron at Redhill when, following a medical examination, I was pronounced fit for very high altitude operations and sent to join the Special Service Flight which was then forming at Northolt. On arrival there, at the beginning of September, I learnt the purpose of the new unit. During the previous couple of weeks the Germans had been sending in single Junkers 86 bombers at altitudes above 40,000 feet, to attack targets in southern England. Conventional fighter units had found these high-flying raiders impossible to catch; with medically selected and specially trained pilots flying modified Spitfire IXs, we hoped to do better. There were six of us in the Special Service Flight which was under the command of Flight Lieutenant Jimmy Nelson, an American ex-Eagle Squadron pilot.

Training for the new role began immediately. First of all we were put on a special diet which included plenty of sweets, chocolate, eggs and bacon, fresh orange juice and other things which at that time were either strictly rationed or else unobtainable. There is now some doubt regarding the effectiveness of this diet in improving our performance at high altitude; but it certainly did a lot for our morale on the ground and increased our standing with the girls!

As part of our training we were sent to Farnborough where we underwent tests in the decompression chamber and had a short course of lectures from the doctors there. To conserve our strength and delay the effects of oxygen shortage at high altitude, we were enjoined to make all our movements slowly and deliberately. Everything had to be done in an "icy calm" manner.

At the end of the first week in September the Flight received the first of the Spitfire IXs which had been modified for very high altitude operations. The aircraft, serial BF 273, had been lightened in almost every way possible. A lighter wooden propeller had been substituted for the normal metal one; all of the armour had been removed as had the four machine guns, leaving an armament of only the two 20 mm Hispano cannons; the aircraft was painted in a special light-weight finish, which gave it a colour rather like Cambridge blue; and all equipment not strictly necessary for high altitude fighting was removed. It had the normal, not the extended span, wing tips. Of course, a pressure cabin would have been very nice; but the Spitfire VII, which was in effect a Mark IX with a pressure cabin, was not yet ready for operations.

On September 10th I made my first flight in the modified Spitfire IX and found it absolutely delightful to handle; during the war I flew eleven different versions of the Spitfire and this was far and away the best. The 450-pound reduction in weight was immediately noticeable once one was airborne and with the Merlin 61 she had plenty of power and was very lively. I made a second flight that day to test the cannons, during which I took her up to 43,400 feet. I stayed above 40,000 feet for some time and found it quite exhilarating: it was a beautiful day and I could see along the coast of England from Dover to Plymouth, and almost the whole of the northern coast of France as far as Belgium and Holland. During this flight I wore an electrically heated flying suit, which kept me warm and comfortable.

On September 12th I made my second high altitude flight and this time it was in earnest. That morning it had been my turn to wait at readiness and at 09.27 hours I was scrambled to meet an aircraft being watched on radar climbing to height over France; it looked suspiciously like another one of the high-flying raiders.

Climbing away at full throttle, the Spitfire went up like a lift; but there was a long way to go—40,000 feet is about $7\frac{1}{2}$ miles high. I climbed in a wide spiral over Northolt to 15,000 feet, then the ground controller informed me that the incoming aircraft was over mid-Channel and heading towards the Portsmouth area; I was ordered on to a south-westerly heading to cut him off. After several course corrections I finally caught sight of the enemy aircraft as it was flying up the Solent; I was at about 40,000 feet and he was slightly higher and out to starboard. I continued my climb and headed after him, closing in until I could make out the outline of a Junkers 86; by then I was about half a mile away from him and we were both at 42,000 feet to the north of Southampton. The German crew had obviously seen me, because I saw the Junkers jettison its bomb, put up its nose to gain altitude and turn round for home. My Spitfire had plenty of performance in hand, however. I jettisoned my 30 gallon slipper tank which was now empty, and had little difficulty in following him in the climb and getting about 200 feet above the bomber. At this stage I remember telling myself: "Take it easy, conserve your strength, keep icy calm". The grey-blue Junkers seemed enormous and it trailed a long, curling condensation trail. It reminded me of a film I had once seen, of an aerial view of an ocean liner ploughing through a calm sea and leaving a wake.

I positioned myself for an attack and dived to about 200 yards astern of him, where I opened up with a three second burst. At the end of the burst my port cannon jammed and the Spitfire slewed round to starboard; then, as I passed through the bomber's slipstream, my canopy misted over. The canopy took about a minute to clear completely, during which time I climbed back into position for the next attack. When I next saw the Junkers he

ODDENTIFICATION—CXIII

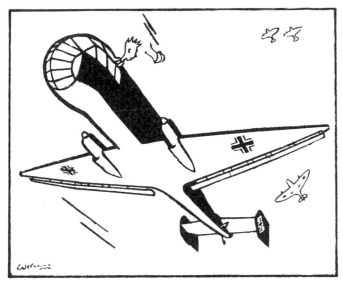

"Than Doktor Junkers' eight-six P there's nothing can fly higher,"
The pilot thought and preened himself until a glance behind
Reminded him that out of sight does not mean out of mind,
And if the sky should fill with lead, the likely clue is "Spitfire."

The high altitude interceptions of the Junkers 86's were commemorated at the time with a suitable ode in 'The Aeroplane' by cartoonist Chris Wren.

Galitzine's hit on the Ju 86R: the single armour-piercing round went clean through the wing from rear to front. *Goetz*

was heading southwards, trying to escape out to sea. I knew I had to get right in close behind him if I was to stand any chance of scoring hits, because it would be difficult to hold the Spitfire straight when the starboard cannon fired and she went into a yaw. Again I dived to attack but when I was about a hundred yards away the bomber made a surprisingly tight turn to starboard. I opened fire but the Spitfire went into a yaw and fell out of the sky; I broke off the attack, turned outside him and climbed back to 44,000 feet.

I carried out two further attacks on the Junkers. On each of them my Spitfire yawed and fell out of the sky whenever I opened fire with my remaining cannon; and my canopy misted over whenever I passed through the bomber's slipstream. By the end of the fourth attack the action had lasted about 45 minutes. My engine had been running at full throttle for an hour and a quarter and my fuel was beginning to run low. So when the bomber descended into a patch of mist I did not attempt to follow. Instead I broke away and turned north east for home. How I cursed that jammed cannon: had it not failed, I would certainly have shot down the Ju 86. As I neared the coast it became clear that I did not have sufficient fuel to reach Northolt, so I landed at Tangmere to refuel."

●

The pilot of the Junkers 86 had been Horst Goetz, on another attack with Erich Sommer as his observer. Soon after the bomber crossed the coast near Southampton, Goetz later recalled:

"Suddenly Erich, sitting on my right, said that there was a fighter closing in from his side. I thought there was nothing remarkable about that—almost every time we had been over England in the Ju 86, fighters had tried to intercept us. Then he said the fighter was climbing very fast and was nearly at our altitude. The next thing, it was above us. I thought Erich's eyes must have been playing him tricks, so

I leaned over to his side of the cabin to see for myself. To my horror I saw the Spitfire, a little above us and still climbing."

Goetz acted fast. He jettisoned the bomb, switched in full nitrous oxide injection to increase engine power and partially de-pressurised the cabin so that there would be no explosion if it was pierced. He then pushed open the throttles and tried to outclimb his assailant but, as we have seen, the Spitfire succeeded in getting above him.

Goetz managed to avoid the four attacks, then escaped into a thin patch of mist. The Junkers landed at Caen so that the crew could check the damage. There was only one hole, through the port wing, and as nothing important appeared damaged the bomber continued on to its base at Beauvais. Now it was clear that the period of immunity enjoyed by the Junkers 86R over England was at an end; there would be no more stratospheric bombing attacks by these aircraft.

The combat between Goetz and Galitzine was almost certainly the highest to take place during the Second World War. Significantly, the movements of both aircraft were tracked by radar sets on the ground; these provided an independent check on the general accuracy of the altitudes stated.

The action had a sequel nearly thirty-three years later, when the author met Horst Goetz at a *Luftwaffe* reunion and was able to put him in touch with Prince Galitzine. The two men became firm friends and together stayed at the author's home to recount their unique battle; later they spoke on the telephone with Erich Sommer, who now lives in Australia. Galitzine no longer curses the jammed Hispano cannon, which robbed him of an almost certain victory but which gained him two good friends. Tongue in cheek, Horst Goetz commented: "Emanuel and I have talked about our battle in great detail and now we understand each other's problems. The next time we fly against each other, we shall be able to do things better!"

Top right: Pilot Officer Prince Emanuel Galitzine. *Galitzine*

Centre, left: Horst Goetz. *Goetz*

Centre, right: Erich Sommer. *Sommer*

Right: Yesterday's enemies, today's friends: Horst Goetz (left) and Emanuel Galitzine pictured at the author's home in November 1975, going through their unique air combat.

SECRET   FORM "F"

PERSONAL COMBAT REPORT.

"S.S. FLIGHT NORTHOLT"

Defensive Patrol

P/O GALITZINE

Personal

SpXO

A. DATE   12/9/42
B. UNIT   s.s. Flight Northolt
C. TYPE OF OUR A/C   Spitfire IX
D. TIME OF ATTACK   1005/45 (approx.)
E. PLACE OF ATTACK   Southampton area
F. WEATHER   Patches of whispy cloud
G. OUR CASUALTIES, A/C   Nil
H. "   "   pilots   Nil
J. ENEMY CASUALTIES in air combat.   1 Ju 86 P.1. damaged

VonR.

GENERAL REPORT

I took off from Northolt at 0930 hours to intercept raid 55 and climbed to
15,000 ft. over the aerodrome. I was then given a vector 240 degs and
told to climb to 30,000 ft. I was next told to fly 130 degs. (35,000 ft.)
and then 190 degs and told that E/A was to port at 40,000 ft. my height
at that time being 32,000 ft. No Hun could be seen. The next course
given was 245 degs. and I was told that the E/A was to port at 42,000 ft.
my own height then being 38,000 ft. Almost immediately I saw black trails
but to starboard, and made off in that direction quickly overhauling the
a/c but I was still below at 41,000 ft. I turned to starboard to
maintain climbing speed and avoid overshooting and came level at 42,000 ft.
with the a/c - which I recognised as a Ju 86P. I was then about ½ mile
to port. The E/A jettisoned a medium bomb (in the Southampton area) and
I jettisoned my reserve fuel tank so that I could gain height. Both of
us climbed again and became level again at 43,000 ft. I got slightly to
starboard and 2/300 ft above and came in to within 600 yds. I dived down
on him out of the sun and from 200 yds. dead astern I opened fire with a
3 sec. burst closing to 150 yds, observing that his starboard wing
outside the engine nacelle was hit. My port gun then jammed and I flew
into his slip stream, my wind screen becoming completely obscured. I
broke away to port and climbed to 43,700 ft. When my screen had cleared,
I picked up the E/A again and getting into position for attack, dived
fairly steeply on him from astern with an A.S.I. of 165. When within
100 yards the Ju 86 did a surprising 45 degs. turn to starboard. I turned
outside him and began to lose height, so I straightened out and climbed
again to 44,000 ft. I again dived on the E/A, who was now flying south
but he shook me off by steering through a patch of thin mist which had
the appearance of expanded smoke trails. My windscreen became obscured
again. Climbing again, I waited until he was in sight and dived on him,
closing to 100 yds. and opened fire with starboard cannon only. This
pulled my a/c round and caused me to drop into his slipstream again with
the usual result - my windscreen became clouded. I had by now lost
distance somewhat but I picked up the E/A again. I lost him, however, in
another patch of mist and he was not seen again. I was now about 25 miles
from the French Coast (Cherbourg area). On instructions I landed
Tangmere at 1100.
The pilot only was seen in the Ju.86P and no return fire was experienced.
The wing root of the E/A was so wide that it appeared to have no fuselage.
I estimate that its A.S.I. was between 100 and 110,
it was very economical in its use of full throttle. I never found
difficulty in overtaking it. In the Southampton area, when I was at
35,000 ft. one burst of A.A. burst 600 yards ahead of me and 500 ft. below,
and after crossing the English Coast intense A.A. was seen below both of
us and ahead.
My A.S.I. was 130 climbing, 145 on the level above 40,000 ft. and 155
diving.

Rounds fired:- Cannon port   25
                       star.   70

Camera:-   not fitted.

(signature).......................P/O..
           S.S. Flight, Northolt

Galitzine's combat report, written after the interception of Goetz and Sommer in their Ju 86R. The 'R' sub-type designation was not known to the Royal Air Force and this aircraft was always referred to erroneously in British reports as the 'Junkers 86P'. It is also of interest to note that Galitzine reported hitting the Ju 86 on the starboard wing, whereas in fact his round hit the port wing.

6

ENTER THE BOMBFIRE

During the Second World War almost every fighter type was fitted to carry bombs and the Spitfire was no exception. The result was the Spitfire bomber, or "Bombfire" as it was sometimes known. The first operations using the Spitfire in this role took place in August 1942, when aircraft of No 126 Squadron flew from Malta with improvised bomb racks to attack airfield targets in Sicily. It was fitting that the Malta squadrons, which had suffered so heavily from attacks on their own air-fields, should have been the first to use the Spitfire in this way.

The following document, circulated in the Royal Air Force early in 1943 as Tactical Committee Report No 33, gives an interesting insight into the methods employed during the initial operations with the "Bombfire".

●

Notes from Malta on the Operational Use of the Spitfire Bomber in that Command

In the latter part of 1942, the Spitfire VC was modified in Malta to take two 250 lb bombs slung directly underneath the two outboard cannons. The reason for the introduction of this weapon was that during the preceding summer the enemy was ignoring our fighter sweeps over airfields in Southern Sicily. Hurricane bombers had been used, and the enemy reacted by sending his fighters up to intercept. The Hurricane had not the same good performance as the Spitfire and made co-operation difficult, especially after the bombs had been dropped.

Flying Characteristics of the Spitfire VC Bomber
The modification to the Spitfire resulted in the aircraft being rather heavy during and immediately after the take-off, the take-off run being lengthened by about 150 yds.

The best climbing speed was 160 IAS at 2,600 revs. The time taken to 18,000 ft at plus 4 boost was approximately 20 minutes, but above 18,000 ft the rate of climb dropped off considerably. There was practically no difference in the speed in level flight, and in the dive the speed was increased owing to the higher wing loading. The aircraft handled quite normally, and aerobatics were carried out with bombs attached and all controls responded normally. One bomb could be dropped at a time, and hardly any difference was noticed in the trim except at very high speeds.

Approach

Approach was made to the target at 18,000 ft to 20,000 ft, and it was found advisable to put the nose down and gain a little speed as the target was reached.

Bombing

The original method adopted in Malta was to approach directly over the target, execute a 180° stall turn, losing all possible speed, and diving vertically on to the target. This method was extremely accurate, but it was found impracticable because of turning back into the flak. Bombs were released at 10,000/12,000 ft. However, over targets where no heavy flak was expected this was found the best method, care being taken not to dive down into the light flak area.

The method subsequently adopted was for the bombers to fly in vics of 3 aircraft, closing into close formation near the target. Approach was made with the target to one side, usually so that it was between the cannon and the wing tip. When the target re-appeared behind the trailing edge, the bombers turned on to the target in a dive of about 75°. They commenced pulling out at about 13,000 ft. The perimeter of the airfield could usually be seen on each side of the nose at this height, and bombs were dropped by order from the leader when the near edge of the airfield was crossed. When the bombs were released, each aircraft jumped upward a few feet, although no reaction was felt when bombs were dropped in a vertical dive. Only very slight allowances had to be made for wind.

The bomb gear was designed so that there was no loss of performance once the bombs were dropped. Unlike the Hurricane bomb gear, the Spitfire (as modified by Malta) threw away all external bomb fittings, with the exception of a steel rib protruding less than one inch from the wing.

Tactics used by No 249 Squadron

The Officer Commanding No 249 Squadron, Krendi, [Squadron Leader E. N. Woods] states that the best results were ultimately obtained by using the following tactics:-

Six Spitfire bombers, each with 2 × 250 lb G P bombs with stick attachments, flew in two vics of three escorted by four fighters in pairs, line abreast. They climbed to 20,000 ft to cross the Sicilian coast. Before approaching the target the bombers formed echelon starboard, and then started a gentle dive, attaining 220 IAS [318 mph True] at about 18,000 ft. The bomber leader flew over the target until it appeared behind the trailing edge of his port main plane near the wing root. He then half rolled to the left on his back and dived down vertically, followed by his section, which were then echeloned to port. The leader of the second section carried out a like manoeuvre with his

section in line astern of the first. The resultant dive was 80–90 degrees. The bombs were released at 10,000 ft, the reflector sight being used as a bomb sight. On releasing the bombs the IAS was found to be about 450 mph [about 515 mph True], thus enabling the aircraft to be pulled out at 8,000 ft, or above the light flak.

Before starting the dive it was found advisable to wind back the rudder bias, and trim the aircraft considerably nose heavy. It was impossible to trim the aircraft during the dive as both hands were needed on the control column. During the dive, the bomber's acceleration was much greater than that of the fighters, which were compelled to

open their throttles fully to maintain their position.

After bombing, the bombers continued their dive to ground level when out of the light flak area, and re-formed in line abreast. The enemy ground defence greatly under-estimated the speed of our aircraft, and the flak was usually found to be some distance behind. In these bombing attacks, none of the targets was more than 15 miles from the coast.

OC 249 Squadron observes that the bomb fittings did not impede the performance of the aircraft as a fighter in any way. With bombs on, the aircraft was somewhat sluggish at low speeds, but fully aerobatic. In some cases

Armourers loading a 250-lb bomb on a Spitfire V, believed to be an aircraft of No 249 Squadron at Krendi, Malta.

landings were made with one bomb on. A much greater accuracy was obtained by the Spitfire bombers than that which our pilots had observed while escorting Bostons over France.

The AOC [Air Officer Commanding] Malta states that some squadrons preferred to break away in a climbing turn so as to rejoin the Spitfire escort. Other squadrons preferred to get away in a gentle dive under cover of the fighter escort.

Top and above: This Spitfire VB was the personal mount of Wing Commander Stefan Witozenc, commander of the 2nd Polish Fighter Wing. The photograph was taken in July 1942 during the preparations for the Dieppe raid. The white stripes were painted on the cowling of this and at least one other aircraft, as a means of identification. *Cynk*.

Left: Skull and crossbones marking painted under the nose of the Spitfire flown by Sergeant Jack Evans (left) of No 71 (Eagle) Squadron. *Salkeld*.

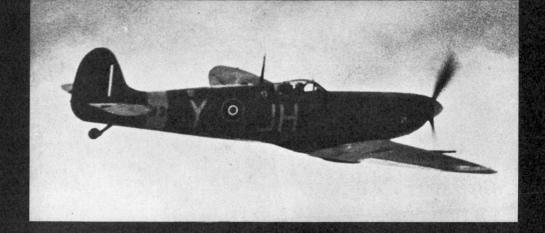

7

SPITFIRE IN SERVICE

Unusual markings.

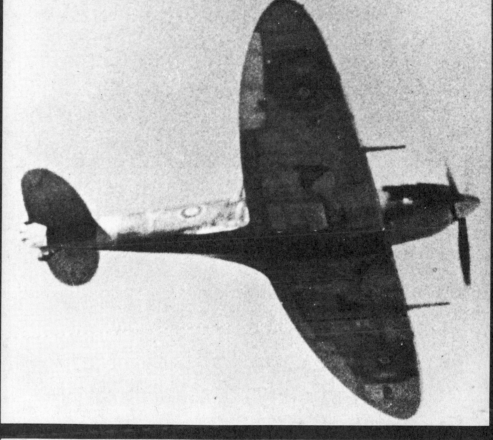

Top and left: Undersized roundels on the wings and fuselage of a Spitfire VB of the Polish No 317 (Wilenski) Squadron. *Cynk*.

Spitfire V's drawn up at North Front, Gibraltar, ready for issue to the US 31st and 52nd Fighter Groups for the invasion of French North Africa in November 1942. These aircraft have had USAAF stars hand-painted crudely on top of RAF roundels, giving a distinctly odd appearance, especially to the aircraft in the background on the left. *RAF Museum*

Photographs taken around the Polish No 303 (Kosciuszko)
Squadron during 1942 and 1943 by Paul Salkeld, the unit's
Intelligence Officer. *Opposite, top*: The Squadron's Spitfire
VB's at Manston in 1942, prior to an operation. *Opposite,
bottom*: Squadron Leader Jan Zumbach, who led the
Squadron from May until December 1942, pictured in his
personal aircraft. As well as his own 'Donald Duck' insignia,
the aircraft carries the badge of the Kosciuszko
Squadron of the original Polish Air Force and Zumbach's
victory tally of 12 1/3 kills. *Opposite, centre*: Squadron
Leader Witomir Bienkowski, who commanded the
Squadron after Zumbach, starting his clip-winged Spitfire
LF VB at Heston in May 1943 prior to a 'Circus' operation
over France. *Below, left*: In June 1943 No 303
Squadron received Spitfire IXC's; groundcrewmen
washing down one of the new aircraft. *Below, right*: Filling
the 30-gallon jettisonable slipper tank. *Left*: Armourers
replenishing the magazine for the starboard 20 mm Hispano
cannon. The drum-shaped object above the gun was the
Belt Feed Mechanism which, operated by a preloaded spring
kept wound by the recoil of the gun, removed the rounds
from the belt before feeding them into the breech.

Floatplanes in service.

At the end of October 1943 three Spitfire V's modified
into floatplanes, serials W 3760, EP 751 and EP 754,
arrived at Alexandria on board the freighter SS
Penrith Castle for operations in the Middle East. The
aircraft were subsequently assembled and service
pilots began making training flights with the
floatplanes from the Great Bitter Lake. When training
was complete the intention was to employ the modified
Spitfires against German transport aircraft plying
between the Greek Islands. The floatplanes were to
operate from a concealed base on an unoccupied
island, supplied by the Royal Navy. A submarine fitted
with search radar and VHF radio was to support the
operations and guide the Spitfires on to their prey.
Shortly after the floatplanes arrived in the Middle East,
however, the planned operations were overtaken by
events. In October 1943 German forces, with strong
backing from the Luftwaffe, re-entered the
Dodecanese and by mid-November they had ejected
the British forces from the islands of Kos and Leros.
As a result the scheme to operate the floatplanes from
an undefended secret base was no longer feasible and
had to be dropped.
In addition to the floats, the modifications to the
Spitfire V's included the fitting of a four-bladed
propeller 11 ft 3 in in diameter (the largest fitted to a
Spitfire), a reshaped fin of increased area with an
extension on the underside, and an extended carburetter air intake to place the entrance clear of the
spray thrown up by the floats. The floats were 25 ft 7 in
long and 3 ft 4 ins in beam at their widest point. The
water rudders were operated by compressed air, controlled by means of the pilot's rudder pedals. The Mark
V floatplane weighed about 950 lb more than the landplane version. It was fully aerobatic, but was about 45
mph slower and had a rate of climb one-fifth less than
its landplane equivalent.

These photographs were taken by Group Captain D.S.
Wilson-Macdonald, who commanded the gunnery school
at Ballah to which the floatplane unit was attached.

Right: A floatplane about to lift off from the Great Bitter
Lake; the take-off speed, 82 mph Indicated, was some
10 mph faster than that of the landplane version.

Left and below: Floatplanes airborne; the extended lip of the carburetter air intake is clearly visible. *Below right*: A floatplane alighting, leaving a line of spray; the optimum touch-down speed was 70 mph Indicated, slightly higher than that of the landplane version. *Opposite, right*: A floatplane drawn up on the sandy shore of the Great Bitter Lake for servicing. *Opposite, below*: Floatplanes on the hard standing, with the detachable wheeled beaching chassis in place.

Above, right and below: On June 19th 1944 a section of six Spitfire IX's of No 403 Squadron RCAF was patrolling at low altitude over the American-held sector of Normandy when, near St Lo, the aircraft came under accurate fire from a 'friendly' anti-aircraft battery. Three of the aircraft regained their base at Bazenville, two of them with serious damage. Two of the remaining aircraft put down on emergency landing grounds in the area and the sixth, this Spitfire piloted by Flying Officer S. A. Tosh, made a belly landing in a field near Isigny. American engineers checked that the area was clear of mines, then an RCAF salvage team dismantled the Spitfire and removed it. *Canadian National Archive*

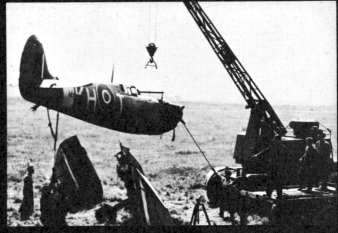

Snow scene: Spitfire LF XVI's of the Polish No 317 (Wilenski) Squadron photographed at Grimbergen, Belgium, in 1945. *Cynk*

An unusual modification to a Spitfire IX of No 312 (Czech) Squadron, to enable it to carry two 45-gallon drop tanks.

Flight Lieutenant Prince Emanuel Galitzine of No 72 Squadron bringing in the first aircraft to land at the newly-completed air strip at Ramatuelle near St Tropez on August 19th 1944, four days after the initial Allied landings in the south of France. *IWM. Right*: Group Captain W. Duncan-Smith, the commander of No 324 Wing, flew with Galitzine to Ramatuelle to inspect the new airstrip after its completion by US Army engineers. This photograph, taken soon after the arrival of the Spitfires, shows Galitzine in the back of the jeep and Duncan-Smith sitting next to the driver. Driving the jeep was Squadron Leader 'Tiny' Le Petit, the senior administrative officer at Ramatuelle. The aircraft in the background was Duncan-Smith's personal Spitfire and carried his initials. Ramatuelle was judged suitable for operations and the rest of No 72 Squadron's Spitfires arrived that afternoon. *Galitzine*

Opposite: Beautiful spy—the Spitfire PR XI.

Reconnaissance Spitfires

Top, left: The clean lines of the unarmed reconnaissance Mark XI made it the best version available for the high speed diving trials carried out at Farnborough in April 1944. Squadron Leader A. F. Martindale flew this aircraft, serial EN 409, in a high speed dive from 40,000 feet to 27,000 feet during which he exceeded a true airspeed of 600 mph (about Mach = 0.9). While he was almost at maximum speed there was a failure of the constant speed drive unit of the propeller and the latter broke away. Exercising great skill and considerable coolness Martindale succeeded in gliding the aircraft 20 miles back to Farnborough and made a normal landing. *Below:* Ground crewmen removing the film magazines from a Spitfire PR XI of the 7th Photo Group, USAAF, at Mount Farm in Oxfordshire. *Left:* A Spitfire FR XIV bearing the initials of Wing Commander R. Wadell, the commander of No 39 (Reconnaissance) Wing, photographed at Eindhoven in January 1945.
Below, left: A pair of F.24 8-inch focal length cameras pointing forwards from a modified 90-gallon drop tank, fitted to a Spitfire FR XIV for low altitude photography.

Spitfire XIV Component parts

1. Engine cowling, top panel
2. Engine cowling, side panel
3. 10 SWG light alloy top cover for fuel and oil tanks
4. Oil tank, 12 gallons
5. Upper main fuel tank, 36 gallons
6. Jettisonable cockpit canopy
7. Stressed skin covered rear fuselage
8. Whip aerial for TR 1143 VHF radio
9. Fin front fairing
10. Elevators
11. Fin assembly
12. Rudder
13. Rudder trim tab
14. Elevator trim tab
15. Tailplane assembly
16. Retractable tail wheel
17. Pilot's seat, with back armour
18. Lower main fuel tank, 48 gallons
19. Aileron
20. Detachable wing tip
21. Port mainplane
22. Port main undercarriage
23. Hispano 20 mm cannon, with 120 rounds of ammunition
24. Browning .5-in machine gun, with 230 rounds of ammunition
25. Wing fuel tank, $12\frac{3}{4}$ gallons
26. Port wing radiator and oil cooler
27. Wing root fairing
28. Engine cowling, underneath panel with carburetter air intake
29. Propeller blades of Jablo ('improved' wood); diameter 10 ft 5 ins
30. Rotol hydraulic constant speed five-bladed airscrew
31. Rolls Royce Griffon 65 engine with two-speed two-stage supercharger, developing 2,035 horse power at 24,500 ft
32. Firewall at rear of engine
33. Instrument panel
34. Laminated glass ('bullet proof') windscreen

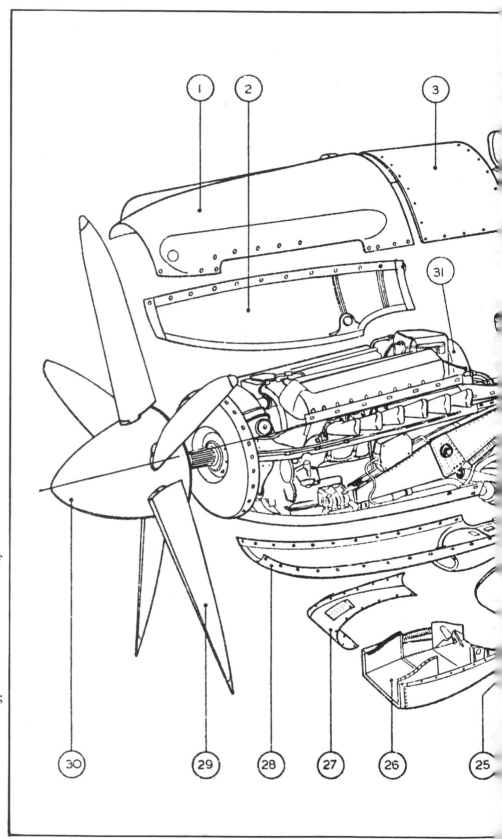

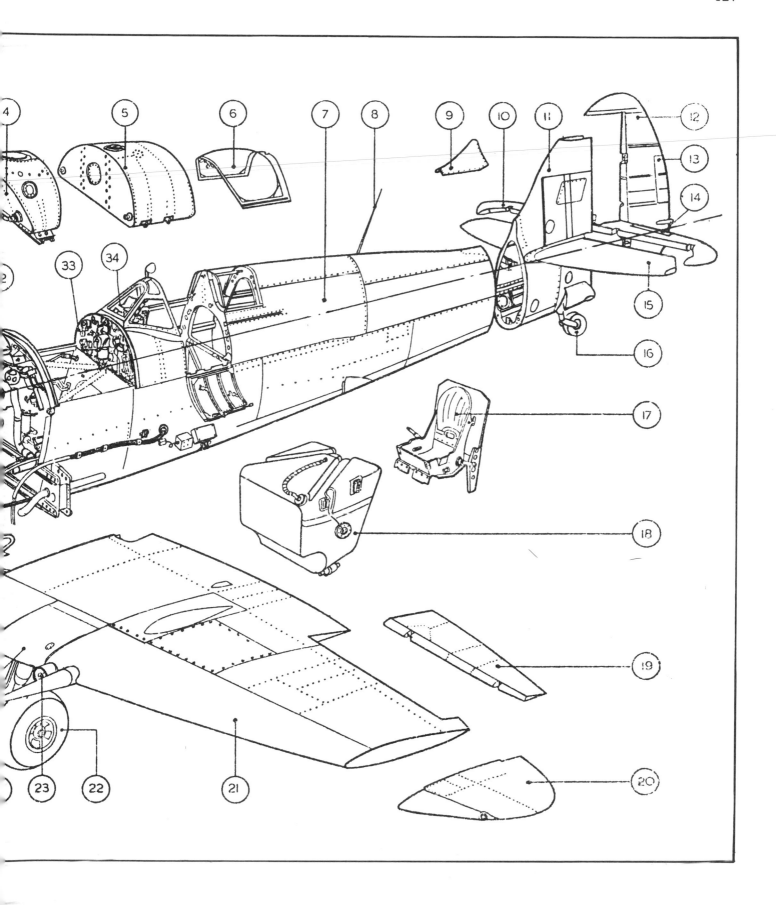

Photographs from the album of Flying Officer Hugh Murland, who flew Spitfire LF IX's and XVI's with No 74 Squadron, 2nd Tactical Air Force, during the closing stages of the war in Europe. During some of its railway interdiction missions No 74 Squadron's Spitfires were armed with a 500 lb bomb and two 60 lb rockets (*left and below*). The rockets were regarded as a poor substitute for the two 250 lb bombs which could otherwise be carried on the wing mounting points, and were not used often. Due to the different trajectories of the rockets and the 500 lb bomb, the pilots had to make separate rocket and bomb attacks on their targets. *Opposite, centre and bottom:* Spitfires of No 74 Squadron being readied for a mission at Schijndel in Holland; the objects at the end of the line of aircraft were 30-gallon drop tanks ready for use. *Opposite, top:* A pair of No 74 Squadron Spitfires landing at Droppe, just inside the German border near Lingen, almost at the end of the war.

8

TRIALS AND TRIBULATIONS OF THE MARK 21

Soon after the outbreak of the Second World War the Rolls-Royce company had begun work on an enlarged engine based on the Merlin, the Griffon. The Griffon had a cubic capacity 36 per cent greater than that of the Merlin but, as a result of some clever juggling with the camshaft and magneto drives, it was no longer than its predecessor and only three per cent greater in frontal area. The first version of the Griffon to go into service in a Spitfire was the Mark III with single-stage supercharging, which was fitted to the Spitfire XII low altitude fighter which became operational early in 1943; the engine weighed 1,980 pounds for an output of 1,735 horse power (compared with 1,385 pounds for 1,470 horse power for the broadly equivalent Merlin 45). The airframes for the initial production versions of the Spitfire XII were essentially those of Mark Vs modified to take the larger engine.

The next stage in the development of the Griffon was to fit two-stage supercharging, to improve high altitude performance. The first version to incorporate this was the Griffon 61 which weighed 2,090 pounds for an output of 2,035 horse power (compared with 1,630 pounds for 1,565 horse power for the Merlin 61 with two-stage supercharging). The Griffon 61 was fitted to the Spitfire XIV, which entered service early in 1944. The airframes for the initial production versions of the Spitfire XIV were essentially those of Mark VIIIs, modified to take the Griffon in place of the Merlin and with enlarged fin and rudder surfaces to balance out the increased torque from the more powerful engine.

While this process of hasty improvisation was in progress, it was clear that to get the most out of the extra power available from the Griffon 61 a major redesign of the Spitfire airframe was necessary. The result was the

Spitfire Mark 21. Almost from the start there were difficulties with this version. As early as July 1942 the C-in-C Fighter Command, Air Chief Marshal Sir Sholto Douglas, was moved to write in a paper on his future requirements for fighters:

"The Spitfire XXI is an example of an aeroplane which is likely to arrive too late unless engine development and production can be speeded up. Although there is no reason to doubt the soundness of the design, we are faced with the disadvantage that the forerunner of the Griffon 61, ie the Griffon IIB, has not yet been subjected to the rigorous testing which the Merlin types have enjoyed. Thus it may appear unwise to force the development of the more complicated 2-speed 2-stage version until the earlier model has proved itself reliable. All the same, if we are to catch up with enemy development, production of the Griffon 61 [must be] accelerated and the risks involved must be accepted."

It was July 1944 before the first production Mark 21 came off the line at Castle Bromwich. The second aircraft followed over a month later. In its production form the Mark 21 was fitted with a completely new wing, which differed from the distinctive elliptical shape associated with earlier versions of the Spitfire.

To improve the rolling performance, all-important for fighter-versus-fighter combat, larger ailerons were necessary for the Spitfire. Those fitted to the Mark 21 were about 5 per cent longer than those of earlier versions. The resultant extensions, which added about 8 inches to the outer end of each aileron, meant that the trailing edge of the wing towards the tip had to be straightened out to allow room for the larger control surface. This revision added an inch to the wing span and two square feet to the wing area. To improve the high speed manoeuvrability of the aircraft and to enable the larger ailerons to be used to full effect, the wing was made nearly 50 per cent stiffer by means of a modified internal structure and the use of thicker gauge skinning. Two additional fuel tanks, each of 5½ gallons capacity, were built into the leading edge of the wing close to the root. The wing also housed the armament of four 20 mm Hispano cannon which was fitted to the Mark 21 as standard.

To improve ground handling, the main undercarriage legs of the Mark 21 were placed 7¾ inches further apart than on earlier marks. To allow ground clearance for a propeller larger than any previously fitted to a landplane version of the Spitfire, the oleo legs were lengthened by 4½ inches. Two doors fitted to the mainplane faired off the wheels when the undercarriage was retracted.

The longer undercarriage legs allowed the Mark 21 to take a five-bladed Rotol propeller eleven feet in diameter, 7 inches greater than that fitted to the Mark XIV. As a result of the various changes the Mark 21 was 10 to 12 mph faster at all altitudes than the Mark

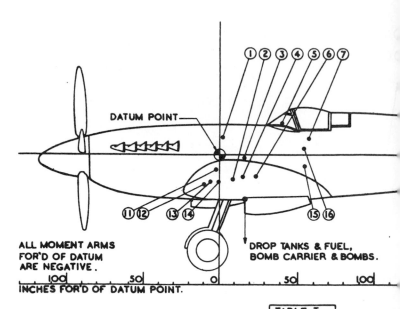

DATUM POINT

ALL MOMENT ARMS FOR'D OF DATUM ARE NEGATIVE.

DROP TANKS & FUEL, BOMB CARRIER & BOMBS.

INCHES FOR'D OF DATUM POINT.

TABLE I

NOTE NO.	ITEM NO.	TYPICAL REMOVABLE ITEMS OF MILITARY LOAD.
1	14	2 INBOARD HISPANO 20 MM. GUNS AND ACCESSORIES.
1	2	2 OUTBOARD HISPANO 20MM. GUNS AND ACCESSORIES.
	4	AMMUNITION FOR INBOARD HISPANO 20 MM. GUNS AT 150 RD. PE
	6	AMMUNITION FOR OUTBOARD HISPANO 20MM. GUNS AT 150 RD
	5	REFLECTOR SIGHT MKIIS AND 4 FILAMENT LAMPS TYPE 'B'.
	7	1¼LB. INCENDIARY BOMB MKI, CLOCK MKII AND CROWBAR.
	13	G.45 CAMERA MKI, ADAPTOR TYPE 32, FRONT FLANGE AND INDICA
	10	OXYGEN CYLINDER MK.Vₐ.
	15	DINGHY TYPE 'K' IN SEAT PACK TYPE 'A' MK II.
	17	FIRST-AID OUTFIT.
2	8	T. R.J143 RADIO AND ACCESSORIES.
	9	R.3067 RECEIVER, DETONATOR NO. D64 MK.I AND CONTROL UNI
	16	PILOT AND PARACHUTE.
		TOTAL TYPICAL REMOVABLE MILITARY LOAD.
	3	FUEL IN FUSELAGE TANKS: 85 GAL. 100 OCTANE FUEL AT 7.2 LB. P
	12	FUEL IN WING TANKS: 34 GAL. 100 OCTANE AT 7.2 LB. PER GAL.
3	1	OIL IN TANK: 9 GAL. AT 9 LB. PER GAL.
4	11	AIRCRAFT IN TARE CONDITION.
		AIRCRAFT IN TYPICAL TAKE-OFF CONDITION.

XIV, even though the two aircraft were fitted with engines developing the same power. Carrying its full operational load the Mark 21 weighed 9,182 pounds and had a wing loading of 37.6 pounds per square foot; these figures compared with 8,490 pounds and 35 pounds per square foot, respectively, for the Mark XIV.

With so many major changes to its airframe, it is not surprising that the Mark 21 handled rather differently

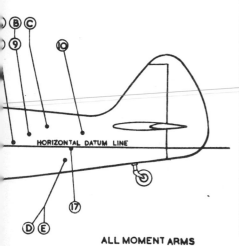

B C
9
10
17
D E

HORIZONTAL DATUM LINE

ALL MOMENT ARMS
AFT OF DATUM
ARE POSITIVE.

150   200   250
INCHES AFT OF DATUM POINT.

	WEIGHT LB.	ARM IN.	MOMENT LB.IN.
	290.5	- 0.5	- 145
	290	+ 8.5	+ 2,465
	187.5	+ 14	+ 2,625
GUN.	187.5	+ 23	+ 4,313
	4.5	+ 40	+ 180
	3	+ 58	+ 174
PE 45.	7	- 5.5	- 39
	19.5	+187	+ 3,647
	15	+ 55	+ 825
	2.5	+175.5	+ 439
	79.5	+142	+11,289
BLY TYPE 1.	35	+151.5	+ 5,302
	200	+ 55	+11,000
	1,321.5		+42,075
	612	+ 15.5	+ 9,486
	245	- 9.5	- 2,328
	81	+ 1	+ 81
	6,923		-14,607
	9,182.5	+ 3.8	+34,707

TABLE II

DROP TANKS AND FUEL, BOMB CARRIER AND BOMBS.	WEIGHT LB.	ARM IN.	MOMENT LB.IN.
30 GAL. DROP TANK.	60	+ 16	+ 960
30 GAL. FUEL IN DROP TANK.	216	+ 16	+ 3,456
45 GAL. BLISTER TYPE DROP TANK.	80	+ 13.5	+ 1,080
45 GAL. FUEL IN BLISTER TYPE DROP TANK.	324	+ 13.5	+ 4,374
90 GAL. BLISTER TYPE DROP TANK.	120	+ 16	+ 1,920
90 GAL. FUEL IN BLISTER TYPE DROP TANK.	648	+ 13.5	+ 8,748
BOMB CARRIER AND ADAPTOR.	55	+ 18	+ 990
250 LB. BOMB.	250	+ 12	+ 3,000
500 LB. BOMB.	500	+ 12	+ 6,000

TABLE III

NOTE NO.	ITEM NO.	ADDITIONAL AND ALTERNATIVE ITEMS OF REMOVABLE MILITARY LOAD.	WEIGHT LB.	ARM IN.	MOMENT LB.IN.
	B	R.3002 RECEIVER, DETONATOR NO. D39 AND CONTROL UNIT.	32.5	+151	+ 4,908
	A	A.1271 AMPLIFIER.	4.5	+131.5	+ 592
	C	1½IN SIGNAL DISCHARGER, CONTROL AND 6 CARTRIDGES.	13	+164	+ 2,132
	D	1 STANDARD BALLAST WEIGHT ON MOUNTING AT AFT DOOR.	17.5	+175.5	+ 3,071
	E	DETACHABLE BALLAST MOUNTING AT AFT DOOR.	5	+175.5	+ 878

NOTES.

1. ITEMS 14 & 2 EACH INCLUDE 2 HISPANO 20MM. GUNS NO. 5 MKII, BELT FEED MECHANISMS MK1, REMOVABLE PARTS OF MOUNTINGS, PNEUMATIC FIRING UNITS MKII AND ARMOURED FIRING HOSES
2. ITEM 8 INCLUDES T.R.1143 TRANSMITTER-RECEIVER AND CRYSTAL UNIT, MOUNTING TRAY, POWER UNIT TYPE 15, ELECTRIC CONTROLLER TYPE 3.
3. ITEM 1 INCLUDES OIL IN TANK ONLY. THE OIL CONTAINED IN THE ENGINE, COOLERS, PIPING, ETC. IS INCLUDED IN THE TARE WEIGHT.
4. ITEM 11, THE TARE WEIGHT, IS FOR AIRCRAFT FITTED WITH A ROTOL 5 BLADE (WOOD) PROPELLER.

MAXIMUM PERMISSIBLE ALL-UP (I.E. TAKE-OFF) WEIGHT FOR ALL FORMS OF FLYING....9,250 LB.

PROVISIONAL C.G. LIMITS FOR ALL FORMS OF FLYING..........FROM 1.0IN. TO 4.0IN. AFT OF DATUM.

Loading diagram for the Spitfire 21. Each item of removable equipment had to be considered as a weight (measured in pounds) with an arm (measured in inches forward or aft of the datum point). Multiplying the weight by the arm gave the moment (in pounds/inches). If, say, the oxygen cylinder was removed from the rear fuselage, either 17.5 pounds of lead ballast had to be fitted in its place or else an equivalent 3,275 pounds/inches had to be removed from forward of the datum point if the aircraft was to be flown without any alteration in the position of its centre of gravity.

from its predecessors. During the late autumn of 1944 the fifteenth production Mark 21, serial No LA 201, was sent to the Air Fighting Development Squadron at Wittering for its tactical trials. These trials, flown with the aircraft carrying its full operational load, revealed several disquieting features. The resultant report, which went out over the signature of Wing Commander W. F. Blackadder, described the handling of LA 201 in the air as follows:

Take-Off

Full port rudder trim, ie control wound right back, is used for take-off and the throttle should be opened slowly as the aircraft swings to starboard, although not so badly as the Spitfire XIV. This swing can be held easily on the rudder. Except on very short runways it should not be necessary to exceed +8 lbs boost at maximum revs (2750) as the take-off run is short, being approximately 500 yards at this throttle setting and 400 yards at +12 lbs boost (take-off) setting. Immediately after take-off the retrimming necessary in yaw and the extreme sensitiveness of the elevator control make it difficult to hold the aircraft in a steady climb until a speed of 180 mph IAS is reached and careful flying and attention to trim is necessary.

One of the initial production Spitfire Mark 21's, photographed in October 1944 before the unpleasant handling characteristics described in the text had been cured.

Landing

Landing is perfectly straightforward and the actual touchdown is more easy than with previous marks of Spitfire as the wider undercarriage and greater weight helps to keep the aircraft on the ground.

Flying Controls

The aircraft is unstable in the yawing plane, especially at altitude and at high speeds. The rudder is extremely sensitive to small movements and very careful flying is necessary to avoid skidding and slipping.

Aileron control is light and positive at all heights and at all speeds up to 350 [mph] IAS. Above this speed the ailerons tend to stiffen, the deterioration being more rapid above 400 [mph] IAS but nevertheless they are the best yet encountered on any mark of Spitfire.

Although the elevator control is positive in action and the aircraft is stable in pitch, constant correction is necessary, particularly at low speed and at high altitude at all speeds.

Trimming tabs are provided for rudder and elevators. Trimming is at all times extremely critical, and harsh use of the trimming tabs is to be avoided. Reaction to acceleration in the dive, deceleration in the climb and change of throttle is marked.

General Handling

Whilst this aircraft is not unstable in pitch, above 25,000 ft the instability in yaw makes it behave as if it were unstable about all three axes. Because of its higher wing loading the high speed stall comes in earlier than with other marks of Spitfire and in a steep turn the general feeling of instability, combined with its critical trimming qualities, is unpleasant. The control characteristics are such that this aircraft is most difficult to fly accurately and compares most unfavourably with other modern fighters.

Search and Sighting View

The all-round search view from the pilot's cockpit is good although, as with the Spitfire XIV, the view straight ahead is poor due to the longer nose of the aircraft. No trouble was experienced with misting-up of the front panel. The sighting view is similar to the Spitfire XIV and gives 4° view over the nose as against $3\frac{1}{2}$° on the Spitfire IX.

Low Flying

At low altitude in conditions of bad visibility, the comparatively poor view from the cockpit and the feeling of instability makes this aircraft almost dangerous to fly. It is far too sensitive on the elevator and the slightest twitch by the pilot is sufficient to cause a loss or gain in height. In conditions of good visibility the accurate flying which is at all times necessary still limits the pilot's ability to search.

Aerobatics

The aerobatic qualities of this aircraft may seem good on the first impression because of the excellent aileron control, but in fact the instability and constant trimming required more than outweigh this advantage and make the aircraft less easy for aerobatics than previous Spitfires.

Formation Flying

This aircraft is less easy to fly in formation than any other modern fighter; formation becomes increasingly difficult at altitude.

Operational Ceiling

The height at which the rate of climb fell below 1,000 ft/min was 36,500 ft.

Night Flying

The aircraft was flown in moonlight conditions only and without blinkers fitted. The exhaust glare did not interfere with taxying but for landing it was necessary to keep the engine running fairly fast as the exhaust glow and stream of sparks was pronounced with engine throttled right back. The exhaust glow could be easily seen from the ground at a range of 1,000 feet and for dark conditions it would be necessary to fit blinkers. Apart from the stability and trimming qualities already mentioned, the aircraft was comparatively easy to fly and land.

Instrument Flying

Owing to the pronounced sensitivity of the elevator control the aircraft is difficult to fly on instruments; this difficulty would be exaggerated to outside members of a formation, who would also be upset by the considerable alterations in the yawing plane caused by sudden movements of the throttle.

Sighting Platform

The good aileron control of the Spitfire 21 enables the pilot to anticipate the manoeuvres of any other fighter, but due to lack of stability it is difficult to hold the sight on the target, especially when changes of direction are rapid. The effects of instability on the aircraft as a sighting platform will be more pronounced when it is fitted with a gyro gun sight.

It can be flown accurately enough for ground attack purposes in the hands of an experienced pilot and under trial conditions but the elimination of skid is more difficult with this aircraft than with any other modern fighter and makes it unsuitable for the ground attack role.

The report ended with a firm rejection of the Mark 21 Spitfire in its current form for service use:

CONCLUSIONS

The Spitfire 21 possesses the following advantages over the Spitfire XIV:-
(i) It has a slightly greater range.
(ii) It is faster at all heights by some 10 to 12 mph
(iii) It has slightly better acceleration in the dive.
(iv) It has better aileron control at speeds above 300 mph.
(v) It has greater fire power.

The instability in the yawing plane and the critical trimming characteristics of this aircraft make it difficult to fly accurately under the easiest conditions and as a sighting platform it is unsatisfactory both for air to air gunnery and ground attack. Its handling qualities compare unfavourably with all earlier marks of Spitfire and with other modern fighters and more than nullify its advantages in performance in fire power.

The Spitfire XIV is a better all round fighter than the Spitfire 21. The handling qualities of successive marks of the basic Spitfire design have gradually deteriorated until, as exemplified in the Spitfire 21, they prejudice the pilot's ability to exploit the increased performance.

RECOMMENDATIONS

It is recommended that the Spitfire 21 be withdrawn from operations until the instability in the yawing plane has been removed and that it be replaced by the Spitfire XIV or Tempest V until this can be done.

If this is not possible then it must be emphasised that, although the Spitfire 21 is not a dangerous aircraft to fly, pilots must be warned of its handling qualities and in its present state it not likely to prove a satisfactory fighter.

No further attempts should be made to perpetuate the Spitfire family.

The Spitfire had indeed moved a long way since the flight trials of the prototype in 1936! The findings of the Air Fighting Development Squadron were confirmed during handling trials with the Mark 21 carried out

A Spitfire 21 bearing the DL code letters of No 91 Squadron, the only unit to use this version in action. *Arnold*

independently at the Aircraft and Armament Experimental Establishment at Boscombe Down. As might be expected, the highly critical reports from service pilots caused a considerable stir. Tooling-up for the mass production of the Mark 21 was already well advanced, to meet orders placed for more than 3,000 of this version.

The task of isolating the faults of the Mark 21 airframe, and curing each one in turn, went forward at the highest priority both at the company and the service trials establishments. The root cause of the problems was found to be over-control, and in each case modifications to the controls provided the cure. The over-control in the rudder sense was cured by removing the balance action of the rudder trim tab. The over-control in the elevator sense was cured by reducing the gearing to the elevator trim tab by 50 per cent and by fitting metal-covered elevators with rounded-off horn balances of slightly reduced area.

The modifications were incorporated on aircraft LA 215, which showed an immediate improvement during the second series of Air Fighting Development Squadron trials in March 1945. The report on these concluded:

The critical trimming characteristics reported on the production Spitfire 21 have been largely eliminated by the modifications carried out to this aircraft. Its handling qualities have benefited to a corresponding extent and it is now considered suitable both for instrument flying and low flying.

It is considered that the modifications to the Spitfire 21 make it a satisfactory combat aircraft for the average pilot.

RECOMMENDATIONS

It is recommended that the modifications carried out on the Spitfire 21 tested be incorporated immediately in all production models, including the present Squadron equipped, and that the aircraft is then cleared for operational flying.

The "present Squadron equipped" with the Mark 21 was No 91 at Manston, which had started to receive this version in place of the Mark XIV. Early in April the Squadron, its aircraft modified, was declared operational and on 8th it moved to Ludham in Norfolk, taking with it a full complement of eighteen Spitfire 21s.

Operational missions with the Mark 21 began two days later, on April 10th. That morning two of these Spitfires carried out an uneventful armed reconnaissance over the area round The Hague in Holland from which V2 rockets were being launched against London. The section of four Mark 21s led by Flight Lieutenant H. Johnson later in the day was less fortunate. They carried out a strafing attack on ships off the Dutch coast but the German sailors reacted so fiercely that two of the Spitfires were shot down into the sea. Both of the pilots, Flight Lieutenant A. Cruickshank and Flying Officer H. Faulkner, boarded their dinghies successfully and were later picked up by a US Navy Catalina flying boat.

Following this inauspicious start to the operational career of the Mark 21, the Squadron settled down to flying armed reconnaissance missions over Holland and patrols off the coast looking for German midget submarines. The latter were active against Allied shipping in the area and in the approaches to Antwerp. At midday on April 26th the Mark 21s scored a rare success when Flight Lieutenants W. Marshal and J. Draper caught one of the midget U-boats as it was putting out from The Hook. The intelligence report issued after the incident stated:

AI/160 Secret Report on Midget Sub Attack 26 April 1945

Red Section 91 Sqn, two Spits XXI F/Lt W. C. Marshall and F/Lt J. W. P. Draper D. F. C. (Canadian) were airborne at 1035 hrs on April 26th 1945 on anti-midget submarine patrol which they carried out uneventfully from 1100/1200 hrs. Having flown the last leg down to the Schelde Red 1 decided to return to base from The Hague, but while flying northwards to that point Red 2 (F/Lt Draper) sighted a midget submarine of the *Biber* type heading out to sea just off the mole at The Hook. Red 2 informed Red 1 by R/T and turned 180 degrees to attack followed by Red 1. Time 1205 hrs. The midget sub was then some 250/300 yards off shore and despite moderate but accurate light flak from gun positions on the mole, the section attacked with cannon in dives 1000/50 feet obtaining strikes on the superstructure around the conning tower which brought the sub almost to a standstill. The Section made a second attack this time in a northerly direction from the same height. Strikes were again scored and as a result of this second attack the sub was seen to sink leaving some wreckage and a large patch of oil on the surface. Both pilots fired a short burst on the oil patch and then set course for base landing at 1230 hours claiming the midget submarine as destroyed. Another Section of 91 Sqn subsequently sighted a red cross lifeboat searching the vicinity of the attack obviously looking for survivors.

The 6-ton *Biber* one-man midget submarine, one of which was attacked by Flight Lieutenants Draper and Marshal on April 26th 1945. These boats had a maximum safe diving depth of only 65 feet, and the pressure hull was not thick enough to resist hits from 20 mm armour piercing rounds. *via Selinger*

Between April 10th 1945 and the end of the war in Europe less than a month later, No 91 Squadron flew a total of 154 operational sorties with the Mark 21 for the loss of two aircraft, both on the first day. At this stage of the war targets were hard to come by, especially for the home-based fighter squadrons. Apart from the incidents described the Mark 21s had little opportunity to fire their guns in anger. However the missions flown by No 91 Squadron off the Dutch coast and the destruction of the *Biber* allow an addition to be made to the lengthy list of tasks successfully performed by the Spitfire: that of anti-submarine patrol aircraft.

Even though its initial handling problems had been sorted out early in 1945, only 120 production Spitfire 21's were completed; and all of these were to the original contract signed in May 1942. During 1943 and 1944 the Air Ministry placed additional contracts for more than 3,000 Mark 21s but these were either cancelled at the end of the war or amended to cover the construction of other versions of the Spitfire or Seafire. The first generation jet fighters had an overwhelmingly better performance than the final versions of the Spitfire; the time had come for something better.

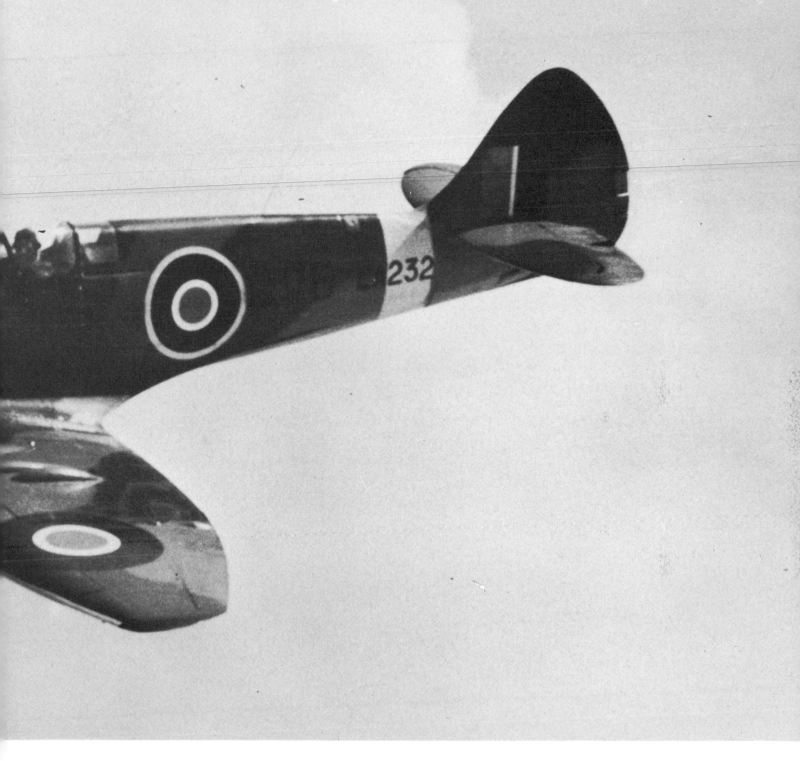

Once the handling problems of the Mark 21 were sorted out the version became popular, especially the few which went into service fitted with contra-rotating propellers. The latter did away with the problem of engine torque, which assumed serious proportions in the final generation of piston-engined fighters. The contra-rotating propeller was a hefty item, however, involving some 300 lbs of extra weight on the extreme nose which required either a shift of equipment or about 100 lb of lead ballast in the tail to balance the aircraft; significantly, no other type of fighter (except for the Seafire) entered service fitted with this type of airscrew. The Mark 21 with the contra-rotating airscrew depicted was the personal machine of Air Vice-Marshal J. W. Baker, the commander of No 12 Group in 1946; the aircraft bears his initials on the rear fuselage, behind the roundel. *Moxon*

9.

TIME FOR SOMETHING BETTER

By the end of the Second World War the Spitfire had reached virtually the end of its development life. In its final fighter versions it was as good as any piston-engined type; but by 1945 the end was in sight for the piston engine as a power plant for fighter aircraft. Compared with the piston engine, the turbo-jet offered greater power for less weight. More important, the thrust from the turbo-jet increased with speed; this was in contrast to the thrust generated by a rotating propeller, which decreased as it became progressively less efficient at the higher forward speeds.

The measure of the improvement brought about by the turbo-jet engine can be seen from a comparison between the Spitfire XIV and the Vampire I, the type which replaced it in several Royal Air Force squadrons. For a piston-engined fighter the Spitfire XIV was certainly no slouch; yet in almost every aspect of performance of significance in aerial combat it was outclassed by the Vampire I. The trial described was flown during the summer of 1946, at the Central Fighter Establishment at West Raynham.

●

Vampire I v. Spitfire XIV

In making a comparison between the Vampire and the Spitfire XIV, the properties of their engines must be realised. A piston engine maintains power throughout the

---

The Mark XIV, one of the fastest versions of the Spitfire, was certainly no slouch for a piston-engined aircraft. It was, however, thoroughly outclassed as a fighting aircraft by the de Havilland Vampire I which belonged to the next generation of jet fighters. *Charles Brown*

speed range, while a jet engine only produced maximum power at top speed. Therefore the Spitfire has an inherent advantage over a jet aircraft when operating at the lower end of its speed range.

The Spitfire XIV used in the comparison trial was a fully operational aircraft fitted with a Griffon 65, giving 2,015 hp at 7,500 ft.

Maximum Level Speeds

The Vampire is greatly superior in speed to the Spitfire XIV at all heights as shown below:

Altitude ft	Approx. Speed Advantage over Spitfire XIV (mph)	
	Vampire with Goblin I	Goblin II
0	130	140
5,000	110	120
10,000	100	110
15,000	100	110
20,000	95	105
25,000	75	85
30,000	70	70
35,000	70	70
40,000	90	90

Acceleration and Deceleration

With both aircraft in line-abreast formation at a speed of 200 A.S.I., on the word "Go" both engines were opened up to maximum power simultaneously. The Spitfire initially drew ahead, but after a period of approximately 25 seconds the Vampire gradually caught up and quickly accelerated past the Spitfire.

The rate of deceleration of the Spitfire is faster than the Vampire even when the Vampire uses its dive brakes.

Dive

The two aircraft were put into a 40 degree dive in line-abreast formation with set throttles at a speed of 250 mph I.A.S. The Vampire rapidly drew ahead and kept gaining on the Spitfire.

Zoom Climb

The Vampire and the Spitfire XIV in line-abreast formation were put into a 45 degree dive. When a speed of 400 mph I.A.S. had been reached, a zoom climb at fixed throttle settings was carried out at approximately 50 degrees. The Vampire showed itself vastly superior and reached a height 1,000 feet in excess of the altitude of the Spitfire in a few seconds, and quickly increased its lead as the zoom climb continued. The same procedure was carried out at full throttle settings and the Vampire's advantage was outstandingly marked.

Climb

The Spitfire XIV climbs approximately 1,000 feet per minute faster than the Vampire up to 20,000 feet.

Turning Circles

The Vampire is superior to the Spitfire XIV at all heights. The two aircraft were flown in line-astern formation. The Spitfire was positioned on the Vampire's tail. Both aircraft tightened up to the minimum turning circle with maximum power. It became apparent that the Vampire was just able to keep inside the Spitfire's turning circles. After four or five turns the Vampire was able to position itself on the Spitfire's tail so that a deflection shot was possible. The wing loading of the Vampire is 33.1 lbs per sq ft compared with the Spitfire XIV's 35.1 lbs per sq ft.

Rates of Roll

The Spitfire XIV has a faster rate of roll at all speeds. The higher the speed the faster the Spitfire rolls in comparison with the Vampire.

Combat Manoeuvrability

The Vampire will out-manoeuvre the Spitfire type of aircraft at all heights, except for initial acceleration at low speeds, and in rolling. Due to the Vampire's much higher speed (ie 105 mph faster at 20,000 feet) and superior zoom climb, the Spitfire can gain no advantage by using its superior rate of climb in combat.

The de Havilland Vampire I which, apart from a speed advantage of 70 to 140 mph over the Spitfire XIV, could also turn tighter. *Charles Brown*

144

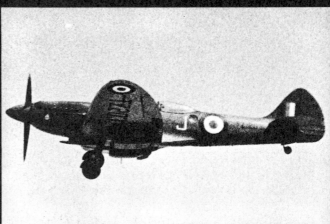

Opposite top: Spitfire IX's of No 208 Squadron based at Ein Shemer, Palestine, in 1947. The aircraft nearer the camera had been locally-modified for the fighter reconnaissance role by the installation of an oblique-mounted camera in the rear fuselage. *Centre and bottom, opposite*: During 1947 No 208 Squadron re-equipped with Spitfire FR 18's and following the end of the Palestine mandate the unit operated from Fayid in the Suez Canal Zone. *Below*: Not what they might seem: clipped-winged Spitfire XVI's of No 17 Squadron painted as yellow-nosed Messerschmitt 109's for the Royal Air Force Display at Farnborough in July 1950. *Charles Brown*

Spitfires Post-War.

Above: Ground running a Spitfire 18 of No 60 Squadron at Kuala Lumpur, Malaya. This unit operated its Spitfires against guerillas during the Malayan emergency until January 1951. *Below:* Just visible on the fuselage of this Spitfire 22 are the blue bars of No 73 Squadron, the only regular unit to equip fully with this version. No 73 Squadron operated Mark 22's from Takali, Malta, from November 1947 until October 1948. The Mark 22 was essentially a Mark 21 with a cut-back rear fuselage and 'tear drop' hood with, in its production form, an enlarged fin and rudder. *Opposite, top:* During 1947 and 1948 eleven of the twenty Royal Auxiliary Air Force Squadrons re-equipped with the Spitfire 22. The aircraft depicted, drawn from Nos 610, 611 and 613 Squadrons, were photographed during a rehearsal for the Royal Air Force Display in July 1950. By the summer of 1951 the Spitfires in all the Auxiliary squadrons had been replaced by jet fighters. *Charles Brown. Opposite, below:* Externally similar to the Mark 22 (from which several were converted), the Spitfire 24 had some internal differences and was able to carry eight 60-lb rockets. The aircraft depicted belonged to No 80 Squadron, the sole Royal Air Force unit to operate this version. The Squadron flew Mark 24's from Kai Tak, Hong Kong, until January 1952 and was the last Royal Air force fighter unit to operate Spitfires. *The Aeroplane.*

STILL A PLACE IN THE FRONT LINE

Although the Spitfire was rapidly replaced in those home fighter squadrons which survived the immediate post-war run-down of the Royal Air Force, the type was to remain effective in the photographic reconnaissance role for almost a decade after the war. The first-generation jet fighters could easily outperform the Spitfire at the lower altitudes; but if it stayed at its maximum flying altitude the unarmed Spitfire 19 continued to be an extremely difficult target. The service ceiling for the Mark 19 is usually quoted as being around 43,000 feet; but the Royal Air Force definition of "service ceiling" is: that altitude at which the aircraft's rate of climb falls below 100 feet per minute. Comfortably ensconced in their pressure cabins, the reconnaissance pilots usually had all the time in the world to get up to altitude and as a result they coaxed the Mark 19 up to remarkable heights. For example during Exercise DAGGER in 1948, the first major air defence exercise mounted by Fighter Command after the war, Mark 19s came in over Britain at altitudes up to 49,000 feet. At such altitudes continuous tracking by the defensive ground radar chain was impossible; the intruders either passed unnoticed or, if they were seen from time to time, there were insufficient plots for even the jet fighters to be directed into position for an interception. During DAGGER eight Spitfire 19 missions were flown; all of them sneaked through the defences, photographed their targets and withdrew, without being intercepted.

The problem of intercepting single high-flying reconnaissance aircraft was recognised at Fighter Command Headquarters which, in 1949, ordered a trial to determine the best tactics to counter such aircraft. If the Spitfires could exploit a weakness in the British defences, an enemy might do the same in wartime.

During the series of trials the Spitfire 19, flown by pilots of No 541 Squadron, ran in to photograph targets at 40,000 feet at speeds around 370 mph (True). The normal operational tactic used by Spitfire reconnaissance aircraft at high altitude was to fly just above the layer at which condensation trails formed; this meant that unless the intercepting fighters were positioned exactly in the blind zone immediately underneath the Spitfire, as soon as they entered the layer and began leaving trails they were likely to be seen and the Spitfire pilot could take evasive action.

To defeat this tactic, pairs of Meteors or Vampires were used during the trial interceptions. Much depended on the jet fighters being able to approach their prey unseen, by exploiting the Spitfire's blind zone below and behind. The report on the trials stated:

(a) The fighters should, whenever possible, approach the P.R. [photographic reconnaissance] aircraft below contrail height with the intention of reaching a position some 4,000 ft below and approximately 2,000 yards astern unobserved and in the process building up sufficient speed to give a good zoom climb. (Both Meteors and Vampires should aim to reach .72 Ind Mach [about 480 mph True above 36,000 feet] before commencing the climb.) At this stage the No 2 should move into close echelon to minimise the risk of being seen by the P.R. pilot.

Opposite, top: A Mark 19 Spitfire of the Photographic Reconnaissance Development unit.

Opposite, below: Ground crewmen loading F.52 cameras, with a 20-in focal length, into the rear fuselage of a Spitfire 19 of No 2 Squadron at Wahn, Germany, in 1948. For very high altitude photographic missions the Spitfire 19 carried two F.52's with a 36-in focal length, which enabled objects as small as a tank in the open to be detected on pictures taken from 49,000 feet. *Flight*.

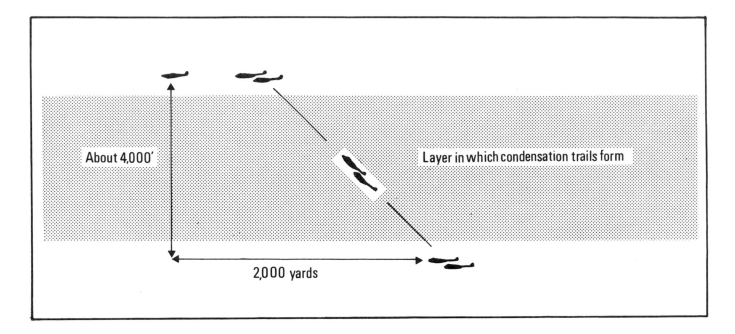

About 4,000'

Layer in which condensation trails form

2,000 yards

Pop-up attack on a high-flying Spitfire 19, as used during the Fighter Command trial.

(b) From this position the fighter leader should pull up into a fairly steep climb at full throttle to within firing range astern and slightly below the target aircraft.

(c) The fighters still have sufficient speed at the top of the climb to close in to firing range. If for instance the climb is commenced from 36,000 ft at .72 Mach with the Spitfire at 40,000 ft and 160 knots I.A.S. [about 370 mph True], the Meteor usually reached the firing position with 170–180 knots indicated [388–407 mph True] and the Vampire with 160–170 knots indicated. Obviously with an attack of this kind it is preferable to close to short range before opening fire. With this attack there are good chances of achieving complete surprise and destroying or crippling the P.R. aircraft before evasive action can be taken.

This type of attack proved highly successful during the trial and enabled the jet fighters to get into a firing position unseen on four occasions out of the five on which it was tried. Its success in wartime, however, would depend on accurate ground radar control to position the fighters almost immediately underneath the reconnaissance aircraft; and this, as we have observed, would have been difficult to provide if the Spitfire had been flying at 49,000 feet. Moreover if the condensation trail layer was thicker than 6,000 feet the jet fighters lost so much speed during their zoom climb that they had insufficient to overtake the Spitfire when they reached its altitude. Nevertheless the reconnaissance pilots involved in the trial agreed that such an approach in a zoom climb was the one most likely to succeed, and the one least likely to be seen before it was too late to evade.

If the jet fighters were seen in time the Spitfire pilot could exploit his main advantage: manoeuvrability. At 40,000 feet the Spitfire 19 had a minimum turning radius of about $\frac{3}{4}$ mile; the jet fighters taking part in the trial, the Meteor 4 with a long range tank and the Vampire 5 without, had minimum turning radii of approximately $1\frac{1}{2}$ and 1 mile respectively (the Vampire 5 was somewhat heavier and less manoeuvrable than the Mark 1 compared with the Spitfire XIV in the previous chapter). Several sorties were flown in order to assess the jet fighters' chances of destroying a high flying reconnaissance aircraft once the element of surprise had been lost:

"(a) If the fighters are seen during the attack the P.R. pilot should allow them to approach to within 800–1,000 yards before breaking hard into the direction of the attack. It has been found that when the fighters are approaching from astern and below, as they will be during the initial interception, the Spitfire turning at maximum rate can only be held in the sights long enough to permit a snap shot with a very short burst at extreme range, ie 800 yards. This takes less than the first 90° of the turn after which the fighter usually stalls and further shooting is out of the question.

(b) The fighters should not attempt to follow the Spitfire when it is obviously out-turning them, but should retain their speed and therefore advantage in climb and zoom which will enable them to break off combat and re-position for a co-ordinated attack from the rear.

(c) The importance of good timing and positioning during the co-ordinated attack cannot be overstressed. If the fighters can approach one on each side of the Spitfire and both get within range at the same moment, the P.R. pilot will be forced to break away from one of them. This fighter therefore has a better chance of following the turn, thereby obtaining more tracking time and a longer burst within range. There is little collision risk for the fighters if one is stepped above the Spitfire and the other below.

(d) Owing to their superior speed and climb the fighters can break off and re-position for a further attack with little risk of losing their target. These attacks can be repeated

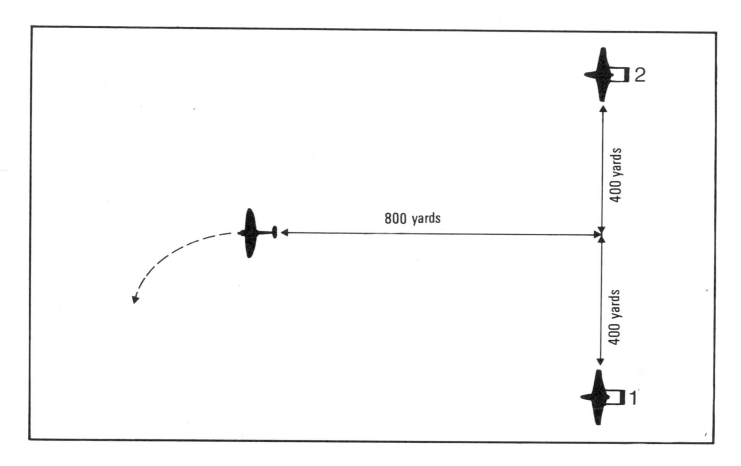

2

400 yards

800 yards

400 yards

1

Co ordinated attack by a pair of Vampires on a high-flying Spitfire. If the Spitfire turned to port to give a difficult deflection shot for fighter No 1, it automatically gave a relatively easy shot for fighter No 2.

and, should they fail to destroy or damage the P.R. aircraft, they will probably drive it down to a lower altitude where it is more vulnerable and will reduce its chance of reaching the target and/or returning to base.
(e) The Vampire proved to be superior to the Meteor when following the Spitfire in a turn at 40,000 feet."

As well as determining the best type of attack for the jet fighters, the trial showed how best a reconnaissance Spitfire.pilot could avoid attack:

"It is considered that whenever possible the Spitfire 19 should operate above 40,000 ft when over defended areas, because the chances of it being intercepted are greatly reduced. This is due to the poor radar response, and the increase in time required for the interception. Also the performance of the Meteor and Vampire deteriorate rapidly above 40,000 ft.

It was found that if the Spitfire 19 lost height during evasive manoeuvres the fighters were able to exploit their improved manoeuvrability below 40,000 ft. The Spitfire 19 should therefore endeavour to maintain, and if possible increase altitude, unless cloud cover is immediately available.

The trial has also shown that the P.R. pilot's best

method of avoiding attacks is to keep a good all round lookout for the fighters, particularly in the direction from which attacks have been recommended. Eyesight training at high altitude is of the utmost importance. It is suggested that an occasional weave by the P.R. aircraft when in a likely interception area will reduce the chances of surprise attacks.

P.R. pilots are well aware of the necessity of keeping out of contrails. When the trails are short and non-persistent, they may not be noticed by the P.R. pilot, but are nevertheless of great value to the fighters. This occurred on two occasions during the trial.

If the fighters are seen when approaching from astern and below, the P.R. pilot can render the attack abortive by making a 180° turn into the fighters while they are still some distance below. This will mean that the attackers have lost the advantage of surprise and will have to climb and re-position for a co-ordinated attack from the rear. During this time the P.R. pilot can either seek cloud cover if it is available, or decide the tactics he will employ when the next attack is delivered.

When the attack is co-ordinated from the rear the P.R. pilot, by watching carefully and making alterations of course before the fighters are in position, can render the timing and execution of the attack extremely difficult. He should, by constant weaving, make sure that his attention is not distracted by one aircraft while an attack is being delivered by another. Some of the films analysed showed that the fighers were shooting at ranges in excess of 800 yards. This was invariably due to the fact that the P.R. pilot had taken evasive action at the correct moment.

Opposite, top: A Spitfire 19 of the Royal Swedish Air Force, showing the ports in the rear fuselage for the split-pair of vertical cameras. Fifty Spitfire 19s were delivered to Sweden in 1948 and the type remained in service until 1955. *Via Hooton.*

Opposite, below: One of the three Spitfire 19's which remained in regular use in Britain until June 1957, making meteorological measuring flights from Woodvale in Lancashire.

" If the fighters are in a good position for a co-ordinated attack it is difficult for the P.R. pilot to decide the direction he should break, but he should not allow the fighters to approach closer than 800 yards before doing so. The break should be made at maximum rate and not continued for more than 180°. In this manner the P.R. pilot can be assured that the fighters will only obtain snap shots at him at long range and though the attacks may be repeated he has a good chance of evading them until the jet fighters' limited endurance causes them to break off combat.

The trial has strengthened the opinion that the level steep turn is the most effective form of break which the fighter aircraft will have the greatest difficulty in following.

Attacks from other directions than those recommended will give the P.R. pilot a better chance of spotting the fighters in the early stages and will enable him to evade them without a great deal of difficulty."

The trial made it clear that the Spitfire 19 was far from being an easy target for the Meteor 4 or the Vampire 5.

Not until the advent of the second generation of jet fighters, led by the swept-wing F-86 Sabre and the MiG 15, were there interceptors with the performance to catch a Spitfire at 49,000 feet; these new fighters did not begin to enter large-scale service until 1949. Moreover, to engage a Spitfire 19 flying at its ceiling the swept-wing jets would have had to use the zoom climb type of attack described in the Fighter Command report; under operational conditions such attacks were likely to succeed only if there was good radar control from the ground (a big "if" so far as the MiG 15 was concerned, if one considers the state of Soviet radar development at that time). In fact the Spitfire 19 remained effective in the high altitude reconnaissance role into the early 1950s and did not pass out of front-line service in the Royal Air Force until 1954.

To continue to be effective for so long in the demanding reconnaissance role was no mean feat. That the Spitfire succeeded is the more remarkable if one considers that the aircraft had originally been conceived twenty years earlier as a short range interceptor fighter, by a designer who had become disillusioned with wind tunnel tests.

In Foreign Garb.

Opposite, top, and centre left: Newly delivered Spitfire IX's of the 51° *Stormo*, Italian Air Force, photographed at Leece in 1946. *Stato Maggiore Aeronautica. Opposite, centre right*: Spitfire PR XI of the Royal Danish Air Force, which received three examples of this version and 38 F IX's in 1947. *Opposite bottom and left:* Spitfire LF IX's of No 322 Squadron of the Royal Dutch Air Force pictured at Semarang, Java, in 1948. The unit operated against guerillas during the armed struggle which preceded the independence of Indonesia. *van der Meer. Below*: A Spitfire 22, one of twenty delivered to the Royal Egyptian Air Force in 1950.

Above: Israel bought fifty ex-RAF Spitfire IX's from Czechoslovakia in 1948 and 1949, and a further thirty-five from Italy in 1950 and 1951. In 1953 jet fighters became available and the following year thirty of the Spitfires were re-sold to the Burmese Air Force. In this photograph, taken at Lod in 1954, the Israeli Spitfires are seen being refurbished prior to delivery; on the far right is an aircraft in Burmese markings. *Cain. Right*: A fourth-hand ex-Israeli Spitfire IX of the Burmese Air Force; this service was using the type against dissident forces late into the 1950s and is believed to be the last to use the Spitfire in action. *Bishop*

NOTE ON DOCUMENTARY SOURCES USED IN THIS BOOK

Part I

The author found a wealth of documentation on the Spitfire in Public Record Office (PRO) Files AIR 2/2824, AIR 2/2825, AVIA 10/8 and AVIA 10/219. Original copies of Specifications F.7/30 and F.10/35 are held at the RAF Museum, Hendon; F.37/34 may be seen at the Air Historical Branch, Ministry of Defence, London; F.16/36 and the report 'Handling trials of Spitfire K 5054' may be seen on PRO File AIR 2/2824.

Part II

The following sources were used:

Chapter 1: A & AEE Report M/692, a/Op

Chapter 2: report 'Me 109 versus British Fighters' is in PRO File AIR 5/1139

Chapter 4: documentation on Malta resupply flights comes from PRO Files AIR 2/7698, AIR 8/980, AIR 20/3026 and AIR 20/5461

Chapter 6: Tactical Committee Report No 33 is in PRO File AIR 14/206

Chapter 8: Documentation of testing of Spitfire 21 is from Air Fighting Development Squadron Reports Nos 150 *et seq*. Report of sinking of submarine by Spitfires is from PRO File AIR 50/91 Sqn reports.

Chapter 9: Central Fighter Establishment Report No 87 'Tactical Trials Vampire I'

Chapter 10: Central Fighter Establishment Report No 246 'Fighter Tactics against Spitfire 19 Aircraft'

Epilogue

The Spitfire was a thing of beauty to behold, in the air or on the ground, with the graceful lines of its slim fuselage, its elliptical wing and tailplane. It *looked* like a fighter, and it certainly proved to be just that in the fullest meaning of the term. It was an aircraft with a personality all of its own—docile at times, swift and deadly at others—a fighting machine *par excellence*.

One must really have known the Spitfire in flight to fully understand and appreciate its thoroughbred flying characteristics. It was the finest and, in its days of glory, provided the answer to the fighter pilot's dream—a perfect combination of all the good qualities required in a truly outstanding fighter aircraft. Once you've flown a Spitfire, it spoils you for all other fighters. Every other aircraft seems imperfect in one way or another.

Lieutenant Colonel William R. Dunn, USAF
ex-No 71 (Eagle) Squadron, Royal Air Force